I Will Die On This Hill

I Will Die On This Hill

Autistic Adults, Autism Parents, and the Children Who Deserve a Better World

Meghan Ashburn and **Jules Edwards**

Foreword by Morénike Giwa Onaiwu
Illustrated by Nathan McConnell

Jessica Kingsley Publishers
London and Philadelphia

First published in Great Britain in 2023 by Jessica Kingsley Publishers
An imprint of Hodder & Stoughton Ltd
An Hachette Company

1

Copyright © Meghan Ashburn and Jules Edwards 2023
Foreword copyright © Morénike Onaiwu 2023
Illustrations copyright © Nathan McConnell 2023

Front cover image source: Nathan McConnell.

A CIP catalogue record for this title is available from the
British Library and the Library of Congress

ISBN 978 1 83997 168 6
eISBN 978 1 83997 169 3

Printed and bound in the United States by Integrated Books International

Jessica Kingsley Publishers' policy is to use papers that are natural,
renewable, and recyclable products and made from wood grown in sus-
tainable forests. The logging and manufacturing processes are expected to
conform to the environmental regulations of the country of origin.

Jessica Kingsley Publishers
Carmelite House
50 Victoria Embankment
London EC4Y 0DZ

www.jkp.com

Dedication

In memory of my ancestors
Dedicated to my children
With gratitude for the autistic community

Jules

In memory of Jan
Dedicated to Barb
Inspired by My Crew

Meghan

Cover Art

Nathan Alan McConnell is an autistic adult, autism advocate, and creator of *Growing Up Autie*, a comic about growing up autistic in a neurotypical world. His works include *Growing Up Autie: Year One*; *Growing Up Autie: The Boy Who Lost His Stims*; *Growing Up Autie: Autism's Most Wanted*; and *Growing Up Autie: Death in Exchange*.

He has published years of free comics, writings, and more on his Facebook page to help family and friends of autistic people understand their loved ones better and help autistic people learn more about themselves, learn to accept themselves, and help fight for the acceptance of autistic people everywhere.

Disclaimers

The opinions in this book belong to the individual contributors. We included citations throughout the text, not to prove facts, but to guide readers to further resources.

Individual contributors of this book do not (necessarily) share the opinions of the other individual contributors of this book. In other words, we all have our own opinions.

The individual contributors of this book did not (necessarily) read the contributions of the other contributors of this book before this book was published.

The publisher and the authors assume no responsibility for errors, inaccuracies, omissions, or any other inconsistencies herein, and hereby disclaim any liability to any party for any loss, damage, or disruption caused by errors or omissions, whether such errors or omissions result from negligence, accident, or any other cause.

Contents

Distractions and Propaganda

And Why Would We Do This?

Can We Start Over?

Let's Get to Work

Where Do I Fit In?

Foreword

⎯⎯ BY MORÉNIKE GIWA ONAIWU ⎯⎯

G rowing up, my brothers and I were fascinated by random science phenomena. We collected and compared different types of wildflowers that grew in a field near our home; made recordings of cicada sounds to compare them for volume; closely observed worker ants, centipedes, and millipedes. We pestered our parents to identify for us the various parts, organs, and bones of chicken, beef, etc. before cooking them, and we spent hours watching various Discovery Channel documentaries and devouring old copies of *National Geographic* magazine.

Sometimes we even examined our urine and feces before flushing the toilet to try to predict what they might look like the following day(s) (i.e. shade, consistency) based upon what we had consumed. And before you say it, *yes*, we were weird kids, and *no*, we aren't neurotypical. (Although I'm the only one of my siblings who is on the autism spectrum, we're definitely a neurodiverse family.)

This "special interest" of mine wasn't limited to the home setting; I was similarly weird at school. I loved instances in which my teachers incorporated interesting scientific concepts into our learning. In particular, I recall an enlightening discussion in elementary school with my classmates and a teacher about a trend that was popular at the time in several movies and video games. A leading character would somehow become stuck in quicksand. The person would struggle viciously to wriggle free, only to find themselves sinking into the quicksand faster and faster...often up to their chin.

However, just when all hope seemed lost and the person seemed destined to perish, they would spot a vine or a branch nearby. They would then begin to thrash and wriggle about from within the quicksand, eventually succeeding in freeing a portion of their arm(s). Finally, in what seemed like a Herculean effort, the person would narrowly grab hold of the vine or branch, clutch it with all their might, and swing themselves free.

Such intensity! Such a struggle!

Such a lie, our teacher said.

She told us such dramatic rescue scenes might capture the audience's attention, but it was not realistic. The best thing to do, she informed us, if you ever find yourself in quicksand is to be very strategic and intentional. Remain as calm as you can and try to be still. Should you have to move, strive for small, slow, deliberate, planned movements, and wait for the quicksand to liquefy. Do not rush and do not panic. Your goal is to be able to move a little, to the point where you're no longer as stuck and gradually begin to float. Once you grow nearer to the surface, try to relax, lean in, and wait. It will require effort, but don't give up, she told us, because in time you will eventually rise to the top and will safely emerge.

I've never forgotten my teacher's words. At the time, I thought that perhaps this advice would be useful if I ever found myself in danger while camping or something. (Fortunately, that never happened.) Upon learning that Jules and Meghan were developing this book, the example of quicksand immediately came to mind when I contemplated what I wished to write in a foreword for a book about the contentious relationship between autistic adults and non-autistic parents of autistic children. It is an especially relevant comparison as you begin *I Will Die On This Hill*. As the authors explain candidly, much of the discord between non-autistic parents and autistic adults is because their perspectives often clash over what is and is not best for the autistic community, who is or is not qualified to "speak" on behalf of others, which approaches are helpful and which are harmful. Nevertheless, everyone involved generally possesses good intentions and is emotionally invested—deeper than the quicksand in those melodramatic movie scenes.

Reader, I get it. Truly, as I live at the convergence of two dualities in which parenting autistic children overlaps with being an autistic person. Sometimes these factors "play" well together. Other times, they seem to compete and/or work against one another. In either scenario, overall society is not as accepting nor as accommodating as we need it to be, and that can be hard. I have learned that being autistic does not magically grant me a sense of comfort if my child is hurting and in need and I can't always discern what's going on so that I can help. Similarly, being a parent of autistic children doesn't automatically conjure up a personal, invisible barrier shielding me from the realities that autistic adults without children face.

I, like my children, have an autism diagnosis, and throughout my years on this journey I have discovered that though autism is a unique entity, and of course every autistic person (just like every non-autistic person) is an individual, autism is like many things in this world in that it's neither a negative nor a positive thing. It's just a "thing." At times, it might manifest as, and/or potentially contribute to, positive and/or negative experiences...sometimes even at the same time. But it is not inherently bad, nor is it inherently good. It is important to realize that regardless of one's role (non-autistic parent, autistic adult with or without children, family member, friend, ally, professional, etc.), with regard to autism, it is imperative to both celebrate successes and to provide support and resources to mitigate challenges. If not, the pressure of balancing societal expectations, responsibilities, values, etc. in a world laden with ableism can erode the strength we need to persevere and/or seek help. This can potentially foster a counterproductive mindset, nonproductive actions, and a sense of discouragement.

When submerged, it's natural to initially react the way one might in many unfamiliar and unexpected scenarios—with confusion, panic, disbelief, anger, or despair. This is illustrated poignantly, and sometimes painfully, in this book, and I've certainly been there myself—flailing about, screaming, crying, resisting. Because I felt controlled by my circumstances, springing into action made me feel less trapped and scared, like I was *doing* something. Unbeknownst to me at the time, the "something" I was doing was only making things worse. Quicksand seldom exists in nature in depths capable of endangering a person's life. Actually, the density of the human body is significantly lower than that of quicksand—approximately one half, in fact. Though we might feel frightened and overwhelmed, quicksand itself does not pose the peril we imagine it to be. The real danger is us; our fearful reaction to the quicksand can entrap us, and we can easily drown if a high tide sweeps over us while we are stuck. The only way to survive is to find a way to completely change tactics in order to get unstuck and become free.

Non-autistic parents of autistic children need to internalize the fact that, overall, autism is not inherently some dreaded, terrible affliction that has "stolen" the lives of your children and mine—even though you might perceive it as such sometimes. Neither is it inherently an enviable "superpower" that makes autistic people superior to others, even though you might perceive it as such sometimes. It's a different type of neurology, and it is a part of your children—and mine—that will exist as long as they do. How that appears and how it impacts their daily reality might look different at age three than it does at age 10, age 15, or age 33, but it is still autism.

Regardless of how non-autistic parents of autistic children might feel about autism, autism ain't going nowhere. No matter how many years of "intervention" and/or "therapy"-one attends, how many gluten-free casein-free soy-free meals one digests, how many "social skills training" programs one completes, how many essential oils you utilize, how many thoughts or behaviors you suppress...your child is autistic and always will be.

Your child's diagnosis will not change, but what *can* change is your perception of and manner of relating to your child, with all their strengths, flaws, abilities, and characteristics—including not only the concept of autism itself, but also the perspectives and communication styles of adult self-advocates from your child's community, the autistic community. You must remember that these adult self-advocates are human beings who might not always say things the "right" way, surviving in an ableist world, who, despite having been repeatedly disenfranchised, discriminated against, and disregarded, are altruistically giving of themselves—their emotional and intellectual labor, their time—all because they care about children such as yours, and they truly wish to help.

Autistic adults need to internalize the fact that, overall, non-autistic parents of autistic children aren't universally whiny, narcissistic "autism warrior" martyrs who resent their children—even though you might perceive them as such sometimes. Neither are they inherently angelic "special" parents who should be lauded for their very existence, even though you might perceive them as such sometimes. Parents' demeanor might look different on a good day when their children are happy, healthy, and in good spirits versus a day in which the parents attended a lengthy, disastrous IEP meeting; or received yet another denial from a program they'd hoped to enroll their child in; or are rushing to pediatric urgent care because their child has an unexplained ailment but is not able to clearly communicate what happened nor express exactly what and where they are hurting. How these parents understand and describe autism might be different the first week of the initial diagnosis than it will in two years or ten years.

Regardless of how autistic adults might feel about non-autistic parents of autistic children, these parents ain't going nowhere—not when it comes to *their* children whom they love. No matter how much advocacy you do and how much you care, that parent and their children are a package deal, period. You share the children's neurology, yes, but you will never supplant the parents' roles in these children's lives; they are family, and always will be.

Your values do not have to change, but what *can* change is your perception of and manner of engaging with the people who matter so much to the children in our community—their families, which include non-autistic parents. You must remember that they are human beings, who might not always say things the "right" way, who are surrounded by hordes of misinformation navigating circumstances in which they have no blueprint and no intrinsic knowledge, all while trying to ensure their children are cared for and have their needs met.

I Will Die On This Hill offers practical, invaluable guidance interwoven with wisdom, humor, and raw honesty to emphasize how critical it is for autistic adults and non-autistic parents to cultivate mutual respect and find "common ground" despite having differing, and sometimes seemingly parallel, perspectives. We must find a way to listen to and learn from one another. This isn't an easy nor a swift path for any of its travelers. It requires developing a sense of humility, openness, patience, and mindfulness. One has to learn unconventional action. To move slowly, carefully, and cautiously despite not having all the answers. To wait, to watch. To offer others "grace" and "space" when they err. To trust in our ability to eventually float up high enough to be less restricted and be able to breathe and move more freely... enough to manage, to cope, and eventually emerge intact, just as my teacher had shared so many years ago.

Whether you are a non-autistic parent of autistic children, an autistic adult, a family member, a professional, an ally, or a combination of these, please heed the words in this book carefully, for it is our actions that will determine the outcome of our community and shape the fate of our collective future. Will you thrash about in vain or will you rise? The authors of this book, and its contributors, have chosen, for all of our sakes, to rise. I hope you, dear reader, will choose the same.

Before You Start Reading...

The autistic community and the non-autistic (allistic) parent community are standing on two hills, divided by rivers of information and connected by bridges. In both communities, there are bridge-builders, bridge-burners, and people who believe there should be no bridge at all. What we must all keep in mind is that our children are standing on the bridges. If we burn the bridges, the children perish. If we remove the bridge, the children drown. The only real option to save our children is by working together to make those bridges stronger.

Over the past few years, Jules and Meghan (we) have been both bridge-burners and bridge-builders. As you'll read throughout our chapters, we began our relationship standing on separate hills waving torches at each other. The rivers we drank from were often filled with toxicity and falsehoods. We treated nearly all of our interactions as "hills we would die on." That's because we knew our children's lives were at stake. We knew the consequences of not doing anything, but we didn't have the tools or knowledge yet to strengthen those bridges for our children.

Today, the two of us collaborate on projects, we speak together at events, and we're co-authoring this book. Jules even wrote Meghan a glowing recommendation letter for Virginia's Partners in Policymaking Program. We'd be lying if we told you a fairytale about the moment we put our torches down and gave each other a virtual hug, although it would make for an uplifting Hallmark movie. But it didn't happen that way.

Our current relationship is a result of what Jules refers to as *productive conflict.* It took the two of us growing individually as advocates, and a willingness to share what we've learned. Each of us had to let go of our egos (on countless occasions) and admit there might be more to a single issue than our own perspectives. In other words, it took us letting go of our black-and-white thinking and acknowledging the gray area that saturates almost every topic we come across. Within this years-long process of growth and learning, the two of us came to the conclusion that there are way more hills we'd die on together than apart.

We write this book with humility and respect for the communities we are addressing. The purpose of this book is to explore the dynamics between the autistic community and allistic (non-autistic) parenting community. We hope this text will emphasize our common goals and provide context to the issues that divide us.

The function of this book is to upset the status quo. Not to hurt anyone, but to disrupt and give sparks of insight. We want to initiate discussion and open a dialogue. While reading, you may throw the book, or you may need to skip sections and come back to them later. All of these responses are okay. Your feelings while reading are valid, whatever they may be.

This book isn't an attempt to sugarcoat our problems or create a false sense of peace. It's meant to guide parents to find autistic adults. It's meant to help autistic people learn new ideas to be more effective in advocacy (not that they have to, but if they want to). We don't claim to be autism experts. We don't claim to be parenting experts. We are simply two people who want to see real change for our children and future generations.

You'll find that this book does not have one singular message. In some of our content we echo one another; in some we conflict. We both have valuable perspectives and insights to share. We hope our perspectives will enrich your own. As with any resource, take what you want from the best of it, and leave the rest on the page.

We invited a few autistic advocates to join us on this project, and their excerpts begin each section. We were tempted to assign each writer a specific topic, but we realized that would limit our book to the topics in our own heads, which would be counterproductive and somewhat ironic. Instead, we gave these authors our book description and we asked them to share a message that they were moved to share. Each contributor in this book is responsible for their own words, and not for the words of other contributors.

The guest excerpts don't necessarily match the section they lead. We think it's more better this way. (*That's a Meghan-ism.*) We are modeling what we'd like to see more of in this world: empowering autistic people, amplifying autistic voices, and celebrating diversity of identity and thought.

We hope this book will be used by professionals working with neurodivergent people. We've centered lived experiences, as disabled people are the experts of their own lives. Our reference section reflects this truth. While we could have used big words to impress readers and critics, we chose to model the benefits of plain language writing. For instance, we found long sentences and separated them into two. We did this even when it made the book less fancy.

This isn't a book to promote toxic positivity and proclaim that this is a time for healing division within the greater autism community. This isn't a time for healing, it is a time for productive conflict. Children's lives are at stake. If we choose to, we can demand equity and justice unabashedly, privileged feelings be damned. If we choose to, we can engage in conflict in a way that builds relationships and invites others to join us in our work. And we can do both, at the same or different times, as we see fit and are able.

This book comes with multiple trigger warnings. Take care of yourself while reading. Thank you for joining us on this journey.

A Note on Language and Capitalization

While we recognize and celebrate Autistic culture, we find that frequent capital letters within sentences might make the text harder to read. For that reason, we decided not to capitalize "autistic" in this book.

GETTING STARTED

Tiffany Hammond

As both an autistic person and a mother, I once felt as though I were in the unique position to bring two warring sides together. Acting as glue, I would bring the parents and autistic adults to the table and they would break bread with one another. A girl can dream, right? I eventually learned that this wasn't what I was called to do, this wasn't my work, this wasn't my responsibility. I initially wanted to join both parents and autistic adults together because I couldn't exist whole on either side. It was exhausting to connect to them as only part of myself.

However, it was even more exhausting trying to play match-maker between the two.

In my time spent on either side of the fence, I learned some valuable lessons, specifically that parents and autistic adults have so much in common but they are unwilling to acknowledge these similarities because they get so wrapped up in the differences. They are so caught up in the struggle for power and dominance. Who is really the authority in these spaces, and within this community?

Parents know their children more than anyone else. They love their children more than any other person can. They will do for their children what another will not and cannot do. They hold special placement within their child's heart that another cannot. They are responsible for their children in ways that another isn't. An autistic adult cannot and will not touch the bond that a parent has with their child, nor will they ever love their child more than that parent will. Period.

But the neurotypical parent does not know autism as intimately as an autistic adult. They cannot experience life through an autistic lens as an autistic adult can. This is something that the autistic adult will share with their children that they themselves, as parents, cannot. And these adults were once children, just as I once was. They have experienced some traumas, just as I have, and they don't want another child to experience what they have so they throw themselves into this work hard, fast, and honestly, aggressive at times because they are passionate about their cause.

Thing is, as parents, we are passionate about our children—and defensive over not only our children themselves, but our abilities as parents. "How dare someone who doesn't know me or my child challenge how I parent?" "Or question the love I have for my son?" "I am doing the best that I can!"

Parenting is hard, and so is existing disabled in a world that doesn't know what to do with you other than toss you aside and occasionally toss you a crumb or two to show you that they "care." Both parents and autistic adults are faced with societal challenges that make our lives and those of our loved ones exponentially more difficult. We are both subjected to mistreatment and ableism. But we would rather take up arms, draw imaginary lines, and plant our feet firmly on whatever side echoes our thoughts on what autism is, should be, and who is most qualified to "speak" for all. Once we find our home on the side of the line, we yell. Everyone wants to be heard, so they yell. There's very little listening and help for one another.

I was once an autistic child, and I know what it's like to be an autistic child, but I didn't know what it was like to be my mother. Not until I was a mother myself. I knew what it was like to be me, but not her. I am now an autistic adult, something my mother doesn't know, but I now know what it is like to be her.

There's a lot one can know about another without shared experiences, but there's a limit. You will hit that point where you cannot truly know what it's like. That's just what it is. There's this space you hit where "you really do have to live something to know something will make sense." This goes for the neurotypical parent of an autistic child who cannot fully know what it's like to be their child or another autistic person, and this goes for the autistic adult who has no children, who can pull from their experiences as a child, but cannot pull from their experiences as a parent.

There are a lot of gaps in our lives that others help fill in. There's a lot we do not know about each other. There's a lot we can learn from one another. There's so much we can do if we work together.

CHAPTER ONE

If Only I Knew Back Then...

— MEGHAN —

He didn't feed the baby doll.

Jay, my youngest child, brought me a snack the other night with some of my favorites—tortilla chips, shredded cheese, and a Diet Mountain Dew. He separated them all out in a divided container because he knows I don't like my food to touch.

Four years ago, when I took Jay for his autism assessment, the clinician asked him to feed a baby doll. Jay never had a doll before. It's not that we were against buying him one, but we had a house full of boys and nobody showed an interest. He looked at the doll and immediately turned away. The clinician performing the assessment told me he didn't feed the doll because he didn't care about the doll's feelings (that he lacked empathy).

I knew it wasn't true. But the assertions that some professionals make, no matter how wrong we know they are, have a way of seeping into our subconscious. They make us second guess all of the wonderful things we know about our children. They cause us to micromanage and scrutinize every move our children make, ultimately losing that time we could be spending on enjoying our kids and nourishing our relationships.

It wasn't until I found the autistic community that I began to unpack and unlearn the misinformation I was taught when I first started this journey with my children. It wasn't until I found the autistic community that I began to start trusting myself as a parent, and trust in my children to navigate the world in their own unique ways. Their insight is invaluable because they too have been misjudged countless times, and they're setting the record straight about these outdated and often harmful theories.

When Jules and I wrote the first draft of this book, we started it in the same metaphorical place that we started our own journeys—at the very beginning, engulfed in confusion and bombarded with misinformation. Staying true to our own timelines, we held back critical information until halfway through the book. In essence, we did to you, our readers, the same thing that was done to us—we stifled your learning by withholding the knowledge that eventually helped us grow into better parents and advocates. We realized this was a problem, so we changed that.

We hope this book will attract readers from all walks of life—from autistic advocates who are well versed in disability justice, to parents who are just starting out, from professionals who want to broaden their perspectives, to curious readers (like my own mom) who simply love to cozy up with a good book. Some of you will know this background information like the back of your hand, and we hope you will smile at the fact that we included it in this book. For our readers who aren't as well versed, we hope this foundation will add context to the chapters ahead.

On Empathy

I started this chapter with a personal story, one that I've heard echoed from parents time and time again. For decades, professionals have claimed that autistic people lack the ability to empathize with others. This damaging and pervasive stereotype is due to psychologist Simon Baron-Cohen's (SBC's) theory that autistic people lack "Theory of Mind."

Before I discuss the problem with this harmful and dubious theory, allow me to define the word *empathy*. Most people don't realize that there are different types of empathy. The two that are relevant in this context are **emotional empathy** and **cognitive empathy**.

Emotional empathy is the type of empathy that most people think of when they hear the word. It's the ability to understand what other people are feeling. When the clinician told me that Jay didn't care about the baby doll's feelings, this was the type of empathy she was referring to. She decided that Jay was unable to understand (or care) that a baby would be happy if he fed her a bottle. The irony here is that SBC's study had nothing to do with emotional empathy, even though it would forever be used against the autistic community in this way since his study was published back in the 1980s.

Cognitive empathy is the type of empathy that SBC and his colleagues were actually researching. It's the ability to predict someone else's thoughts without them telling you. This happens when you're telling someone a story, and you can tell they're getting bored by their body language, so you wrap it up. The person didn't have to say they were bored, you just knew. Another example is when your friend puts a lot of effort into their appearance for an event. You may think they look absolutely awful, but when they ask you how their outfit looks you say, "You look great!" You know your friend obviously likes the outfit and just wants to be complimented, even though they didn't say that.

Out of his tiny, unreplicable study of cognitive empathy (Gernsbacher and Yergeau 2019), SBC concluded that autistic people are not aware that other people have their own thoughts, which he would call *theory of mind*. Accordingly, autistic people cause all of the deficits in communication between allistic and autistic people. And even though SBC himself has come out to backtrack his own findings, theory of mind is still taught in psychology classes across the world (Gernsbacher and Yergeau 2019).

If theory of mind were true, and all of the barriers to relationships and social interactions are caused by autistic people, then what would happen if two autistic people got together and tried to have a social interaction? Logically, there would be double the barriers because there are double the amount of autistic people involved. Both people involved would be completely uncomfortable since they're lacking the cognitive empathy to know what the other person is thinking. Forget about trying to tell a joke or be sarcastic, autistic people don't have the capability of understanding when that is the case.

Enter Damian Milton, an autistic researcher who created his own theory, which is known as the *double empathy problem* (Milton 2012). He recognized that when you put two autistic people together, autistic people no longer experience the same cognitive empathy difficulties. Autistic people create relationships, socialize, and interact with each other autistically. As it turns out, autistic people understand other autistic people just as well as allistic people understand other allistic people. Autistic people simply have their own way of interacting, relating, and empathizing.

This means that the barriers only exist when you are looking at interactions that involve both allistic and autistic people. Allistic people are just as bad at reading into autistic perspectives as autistic people are at reading into allistic perspectives. If the majority of people on the planet were autistic, expectations about relationships, social interactions, and communication would look different. However, since the majority neurotype would be autistic, all of these would be perceived as the correct way, and the allistic way of participating in all of these would be considered deficits (Crompton *et al.* 2020).

So, what does this all mean? Great question! It means that autistic people are all too often scrutinized, studied, and talked about by people who aren't autistic themselves. It means that doctors, therapists, and educators are all too often taught outdated and harmful information. It means that, as parents, we should scrutinize everything we "learn" about our children, even when it's coming from a professional with five degrees and decades of practice.

To put it simply, the notion that autistic people lack empathy is trash. Jay didn't feed that baby doll because he didn't want to. I'm not exactly sure why, but I definitely won't be analyzing his decision ever again... As long as he keeps bringing me my snacks!

The Models

When I first started learning about autism, I placed my trust in doctors and therapists to answer all of my questions. I scheduled appointment after appointment in those early years, hoping to help my children with the struggles they were having. I'll talk more about their stories later. I didn't know back then how many different perspectives there were about autism and disability. I knew that the advice these doctors provided didn't always *feel right* to me, but that's all I had to go on... Until I started learning from the disability community themselves.

It took more than a few autistic advocates to walk me through the **medical model of disability**, the **social model of disability**, and the **neurodiversity paradigm**. Each professional we come across—therapist, doctor, teacher—will subscribe to one of these models or integrate them all in some way. Their ideology, or the way they view disability, will influence the way they view our children and, subsequently, the advice they provide. If you're not familiar with these three philosophies, I'd recommend taking a deeper dive into researching them for yourself. You can find resources at the end of this chapter or in the References. For the purpose of this book, I'll explain them with a story...

Deep down in the bowels of the National Institutes of Health (NIH) complex—beneath the research library, and under the labyrinth of clinical trials, and even further down than the top secret laboratories—there exists a sacred room. And in the center of this room, there's only one item—a human brain encapsulated in a clear glass globe, just like the rose from *Beauty and the Beast*. This brain is no ordinary brain. Oh, no. It's the perfect brain, taken from the perfect human, who did all the perfect things. I'll call him John.

John's development timeline, his cognitive functions, his sensory profile, his academic and work history are all known as *the norm*. The medical model of disability insists that any divergence from John's performance is an impairment or deficiency (Litton Tidd 2021). Professionals who subscribe to this ideology argue that any deviation will ultimately reduce a person's quality of life, so interventions to correct these abnormalities—such as surgery, medication, and therapies—must be put in place.

While the medical model of disability focuses on fixing and curing people, the social model of disability focuses more on accommodations and accessibility. This difference is especially important in the neurodevelopmental field. Autism is a neurological and developmental diagnosis, which means it stems from within the person's brain and nervous system. Many autistic people have co-occurring motor differences and never use mouth words (xMinds 2020). While the medical model might focus solely on speech therapy or surgery to fix the individual, the social model finds alternative ways to make communication more accessible—through pictures, spelling, and typing.

As it turns out, most doctors are only trained in the medical model of disability and have little-to-no training in child development. This is why many of them prescribe interventions that focus solely on outward behavior, without ever mentioning alternative communication options—which is a big problem. When our children are young, we don't know if they'll eventually use mouth words or not, but they *all* deserve immediate access to communication because communication is a human right. I'll talk more about these topics later in the book.

The neurodiversity paradigm is relatively new. It was developed in the 1990s (Walker 2021) and has gained momentum in the disability community ever since. My mind thinks of the neurodiversity paradigm as another model, but in reality it's more like an expansion of the social model. Along with accommodations and services, this paradigm focuses on respect for all people, regardless of neurotype. It argues that there is no perfect brain.

Sorry, John.

Neurodiversity is a valuable part of the human condition (Foundations for Divergent Minds n.d.), but modern society and our value systems have deemed the neuro-majority as superior. In turn, anything outside of the norm is pathologized as diseased or disordered, which is how the medical model became standard.

Modern society has instituted similar hierarchies in relation to race, gender, and sexuality.

Opponents of the neurodiversity paradigm claim that it glosses over people who have higher support needs and makes it harder to access services (Ballou 2018). But nothing could be further from the truth. Being valued and needing support are not mutually exclusive. Degrading language serves only one purpose: to degrade. Dehumanizing our children doesn't help us get services, nor does it promote acceptance and inclusion. Again, we'll expand on these topics throughout the book.

The neurodiversity movement contends that all people should have the support and accommodations they need. Not only are leaders of this movement working to expand services at the legislative level, they're conducting important research in academia to prove the need for these services. In our educational systems, leaders are attempting to normalize accessible practices and reinvent adaptive curriculum so *all* students can participate (Farahar and Foster 2021; REV 2021).

Autistic advocates are trying to change the narrative about autism. The neurodiversity movement values autistic people as they are, without trying to fix them. All people are valuable and should be included. They need support, access to services, and equitable opportunities.

We have the power to change the narrative surrounding autism and neurodiversity. By learning from the lived experiences of autistic adults and rejecting the antiquated rhetoric forced on us by people who *aren't* autistic, we can shift the public's perception of autistic people.

CHAPTER TWO

A Different Lens

— JULES —

I am Indigenous to Turtle Island, Ojibwe matriarch, Eagle clan, colonized, decolonizing, and trying to discover who I am and where I fit in. I am an autistic adult. I am a parent of autistic children. I don't have the option to choose whether I'm one or the other, I'm both. For me, there are no sides to choose from, because if I chose a side, I'd be ripped into pieces. For some, I'm too autistic, for others, I'm not autistic enough. For my children, I'm just Mom. For me, I'm a person trying to live in a good way.

Many autistic people are idealists. We want the world to be just, we have a strong sense of right and wrong, and we may get stuck on "This is how it should be." So, it can be hard to switch modes to "This is how it is in this moment—and there are ways we can help change things to how we think it should be."

For those of us who choose to engage in meaningful and productive conflict, there can be pressure to abandon the idea of working together for incremental progress. I *hate* incremental progress. I want enormous progress, immediately. I want accessibility and inclusion and safety, immediately. And I know that isn't possible in this world. I would love nothing more than to write off the people I feel are unreachable, to shrug my shoulders, and walk away.

But that's a privileged take, to decide that I'm not directly impacted by people whose efforts work against disability justice. So, I take my seat at the table, across from people who think I'm puzzling, rude, and stealing their child's disability resources, and I try to find some middle ground. If I can just nudge them in the right direction, maybe we can make a bit of progress. I'll keep pushing for more radical change at the same time.

The autistic community is experiencing a safety crisis. Autistic people experience unacceptably high risks of education disparities, restraint and seclusion, poverty, homelessness, domestic violence, out-of-home placement via the child protection system, medical kidnapping, medical abuse, police violence, emotional, physical, sexual abuse, and filicide. The risk of state violence is amplified for autistic people of color. These aren't hypothetical far-off concepts to me. This is real life. Within my friend group, I could name someone who has been impacted by each horror on that list.

Advocacy work is painful at times, and I'm moving forward with hope that the future will be brighter for my children and future generations of autistic people. I have cried over failed initiatives, I have celebrated big wins with cake and champagne. I'm here writing half a book in hopes that it can sway every parent into the direction of working towards disability justice because their children matter to me, too.

Worldview and Disability

As discussed in the previous chapter, conversations about autism and disability often include discussions of perspective-taking. Every single person on this earth struggles with understanding the perspectives of others, and it is especially true when it comes to cultural differences. While the models of disability that Meghan described are probably the most well-known, there's much more that goes into our perception of disability.

Different cultures have different worldviews. A worldview is "a collection of attitudes, values, stories and expectations about the world around us, which inform our every thought and action. Worldview is expressed in ethics, religion, philosophy, scientific beliefs and so on. A worldview is how a culture works out in individual practice" (Gray 2011).

The predominant worldview in America is a **linear worldview**, strongly tied to Abrahamic religions, which I refer to as a colonial-capitalist worldview throughout this book. Within the linear worldview, there is a hierarchy of people. Those at the top have great power, and those at the bottom are convinced they must do more, be better, and work harder in order to climb their way up. The cause is hard work, the effect is power. It doesn't take into account any other inputs. If you are disabled, then your work is devalued, and you are denied power.

> A linear worldview is orderly, progressive, and certain, with a beginning and an end. The world can be understood by a cause-and-effect relationship between separate events. (FNEHIN 2014)

Through the lens of the medical model of disability, disabled people are broken and must be fixed. The medical model of disability relies heavily on a colonial-capitalist worldview that values conformity, and those that fall outside the norm are inferior. Disability is believed to be a flaw, defined by deficits. A linear worldview also applies that linear thinking to autism—high functioning or low functioning. These functioning labels are arbitrarily assigned by people who learned a deficit-based checklist from a textbook based on observable behaviors, not based on the first-hand experiences of autistic people themselves.

People labeled as "high functioning" are those who can contribute to capitalism. They can usually speak, can conform to our society's acceptable standards, and are allowed to achieve limited power. Those labeled as "low functioning" do not contribute to capitalism and are deprived of power and autonomy.

A medical model, using a linear worldview, would implement the following process to identify and treat autistic children:

1. Collect social history

2. Evaluate presenting problem

3. Complete assessment

4. Set goals (autistic person does not choose the goal)

5. Provide treatment

6. Measure outcome.

A mathematical formula is often used to determine a cause and effect, which can then be adjusted to achieve desired outcomes. Keep in mind, the autistic child doesn't choose the goal or the treatment.

Throughout this book, I refer to colonial-capitalism, and it is meant to be a gentle reminder that the threads of white supremacy weave throughout the fabric of oppression of all disabled people. Decolonization includes a shift from the colonial-capitalist worldview towards a relational worldview.

A Different Perspective

The **relational worldview** was named and developed by the National Indian Child Welfare Association (NICWA) in the 1980s, though it is an ancient worldview. The Relational Worldview framework was specifically developed to protect Indigenous children, and it's used as technical assistance within the child protection system.

> The relational worldview...is a reflection of the Native thought process and concept of balance as the basis for health, whether that is an individual, family or an organization. (Cross 1997)

The Ojibwe language, like most other Turtle Island Indigenous languages, doesn't have a word for disability, because disability simultaneously doesn't exist and is a natural part of the life cycle. This is meaningful, because our language *is* our culture. Within the relational worldview, people are interdependent, connected to the earth and one another.

The social model of disability argues that people are disabled by our social and physical environment. Disability is a natural part of life. The social model emphasizes the interconnectedness of people, the necessity of inclusive communities, that disability isn't the deficit, that the responsibility to change belongs to society as a whole. Holding a relational worldview, we understand "Disability is a difference to celebrate, not a shortcoming or a reason to exclude people from community" (Norris 2014).

By thoughtfully considering the differences between how a worldview is related to our perception of disability, we discover that our worldview determines who is responsible for inclusion! Why would a disabled person bear the responsibility for their own inclusion? Why isn't that the community's responsibility?

The *Access is Love* project (DIS 2021), led by Alice Wong, Mia Mingus, and Sandy Ho, describes access as a collective responsibility. Access and inclusion are a commitment to disabled people, not a checklist.

In practice, a social model of disability referencing a relational worldview would treat an autistic child quite differently than we currently do. The social model would explore a child's needs in a way that builds trust. Sure, an evaluation will be necessary, but it would be completed in a way that builds trust with the child. Rather than using deficit-based language that makes children feel bad (yes they hear it, and yes they feel bad), evaluators would use affirming, strengths-based language while identifying needed support.

Interventions would be based on helping the child find balance within their physical, emotional, intellectual, and spiritual well-being. Each area of need would be supported, with consideration for the whole child, to ensure they aren't sacrificing one aspect of health for another. The child would be centered and consulted.

Relationship-based models of care would be used to support emotional regulation, communication, skill building, behavioral concerns, and any other area of need. This care would be provided not only to the child, but also to caregivers and other community members.

The idea that one must always be working towards a goal, that a disabled person is never good enough, is rooted in the worldview that someone must always be striving for something more. That work is rewarded with positive reinforcement and new goals. In a Linear worldview, a goal may look like: "This disabled person will become as independent as possible by controlling their emotions on nine out of ten occasions during stressful events. We will support this goal by sending them to daily behavioral therapy. We will reward them by taking them out into the community when they meet the goal that we set for them."

Whereas in a Relational worldview, a goal may look like: "Disabled people will be welcomed and integrated into our community, our community will ensure their needs are met, we will learn from one another, we will co-regulate when distressed, and we will live a good life together. We will appreciate the contributions of everyone and provide the support people need to live a balanced life."

I can't write that on a disability support plan. I've tried, but the white social workers didn't understand or appreciate it, maybe because their "striving for something better" worldview was too entrenched and comfortable.

Intersectionality

As a young child, I attended a bicultural preschool for Ojibwe students. My Auntie was the teacher, and I was very attached to her. Soon after preschool began, all of the students in her class were calling her Auntie. She was always so kind and patient. I had a cloth dress for dancing, it was a dusty purple with tiny yellow and white flowers. I loved that dress and the matching leggings.

At some point in early childhood, I wasn't allowed to go to pow-wows anymore. I'm not sure if there's a specific reason, but it seemed to coincide with my Granny moving out of state. I was raised with implicit, rather than explicit, Ojibwe teachings. I wasn't taught the seven grandfather teachings, but I knew those values were expected of me. No one explicitly told me "There's not a right way to live," but I was certainly taught to reserve judgment of others.

As a biracial child raised by a white father and a Native mother, I was often treated like property, nothing more than an object to be controlled. I was subjected to abuse throughout my childhood. I was raised to believe I was a terrible child. My successes were buried, and my failures were highlighted.

The abuse against Native children and concealment of those crimes is well established. In my hometown, there had been a 30-year stretch during which not a single sexual assault against a Native person had been prosecuted. My own story is no different. As a Native girl with a disability, I didn't stand a chance. Self-determination wasn't an option until I left my family of origin. I first left when I was 12. I babysat for a cousin who worked overnights and didn't go home during the day. This lasted for a couple of years. At age 14, I moved across the country to live with my Granny. Moving in with my Granny saved my life, and I am so thankful that was the path that opened for me.

Throughout school, I heard "She's smart but just doesn't apply herself" at nearly every parent–teacher conference. I could have written the report cards myself. To my recollection, I was never evaluated for any form of disability; I was merely accused of not trying. I was trying. I just couldn't keep up the charade consistently. There were semesters that I'd have straight As, and semesters that I'd have straight Fs, and I could never figure out why, and no one else bothered to try to understand or help. Looking back, it's easy to recognize executive dysfunction, autistic inertia, and burnout. But at the time, I was blamed and punished for my disability-related failures.

Due to what I now recognize as sensory and social difficulties, traditional public high school wasn't a good fit for me. One day, I came home and told my Granny I wasn't going back to the public high school, and I found an alternative school that I would rather attend. Alternative schools get a reputation for being where the bad kids go, but I'd been told my whole life that I wasn't good enough, so it seemed fitting. Ultimately, I finished high school on time with quite a bit of informal support and adaptations from a welcoming community of untraditional educators.

My testimony is only one example of how **intersectionality** affects the disability community. Intersectionality is a term coined by Kimberlé Crenshaw. It addresses the combined impacts of more than one system of oppression.

> Consider an analogy to a traffic intersection, coming and going in all four directions. Discrimination, like traffic through an inter-section, may flow in one direction, and it may flow in another. If an accident happens in an intersection, it can be caused by cars traveling from any number of directions and, sometimes, from all of them. (Crenshaw 1989)

As a young Indigenous autistic girl, I faced gender, disability, and racial discrimination. I didn't experience them in isolation, though. Intersectionality has what Meghan refers to as a "mul-tiplier effect." Discrimination and bias are compounded expo-nentially when people experience them from multiple systems. Disabled people are not part of a monolithic community. We must recognize and fight for the rights of disabled people who are living in poverty, part of the LGBTQIA+ community, disabled people of color, and more. We must fight for human rights in their entirety, and not in isolation.

Racial Equity

There's a broad misunderstanding of equity.

Equity is not the same as equal access.

That's **equality**.

Equity is not removing barriers so everyone has access to the same systems.

That's **accessibility**.

Equity incorporates equality and accessibility, but it goes further. Equity is more nuanced and needs to be incorporated in all stages of planning and implementation of all decisions, systems, programs, and services.

Equity is necessary because the majority population and predominant culture is presumed to be the default across the board. Equity combats the idea that we all have the same values and priorities, and demands that we each have access to services that we have determined are important to us. Equity means considering the value systems and needs of the people being served while planning services and systems. Equity means we stop pushing mainstream priorities on everyone, disregarding self-determination.

Equity isn't about ensuring that disabled people of color have access to the same services that people from the dominant culture have chosen. Many of the decisions that are made that impact the lives of disabled people are paternalistic decisions, made without our input, and exclude us from the planning and implementation.

Predominant culture demands we strive to be "as independent as possible," whereas many of us view "self-determination, with support" as the goal. We live in an interdependent society, and it's okay for disabled people to need support in order to live their best, and most integrated, lives.

The **disability justice movement** was developed by a group of disabled queer women of color: Patty Berne, Mia Mingus, and Stacey Milbern. The movement is fully compatible with a relational worldview. Disability justice takes the disability rights movement of the 1960s to the next level by recognizing the intersectionality of multiply marginalized communities.

One activist group led by disabled people of color, Sins Invalid, developed "10 Principles of Disability Justice" (2015). Among those principles are Intersectionality, Leadership of Those Most Impacted, and a Commitment to Cross-Disability Solidarity. I encourage you, our readers, to research the disability justice movement. I use their principles to guide my own advocacy, and hope that you will do the same.

Key Points

- Information about autism can vary greatly depending on the source. After reading this book, you'll have a better understanding of why that is.

- If you want accurate information about autism, make sure your sources center autistic voices.

- There are multiple ways to view disability. Unfortunately, the medical model is typically the only one shared with parents. Parents would benefit from researching other models, and utilizing resources created by disabled people.

- We must keep intersectionality in mind when advocating for disability justice.

Resources to Explore

Project LETS

   https://projectlets.org/disability-justice

Sins Invalid, "10 Principles of Disability Justice"

   www.sinsinvalid.org/blog/10-principles-of-disability-justice

AWN (Autistic Women & Nonbinary Network)

   https://awnnetwork.org

Epiphanies of Equity, LLC (Online Trainings and Consulting)

   www.christianaobeysumner.com

Care Work: Dreaming Disability Justice by Leah Lakshmi Piepzna-Samarasinha

All the Weight of Our Dreams edited by Lydia X.Z. Brown *et al.*

LIMITED BY OUR OWN PERSPECTIVES

Kristy Forbes

When a child is identified (diagnosed) autistic, there is an initiation process. It often begins with the professional, who bases their practice on the education they've received at a tertiary level. That education, that qualification, is informed by almost 80 years of text-book lines reflecting the work of Kanner and Asperger.

Two white, middle-aged men of privilege—their bodies of work sharing with the world the largely misinformed understanding of autism labeled as childhood schizophrenia, or children who were of elite intelligence coupled with inept social abilities.

Over the span of those 80 years, that same information has been regurgitated over and over, yet presented in different ways— Classical autism or Kanner's autism, Asperger's syndrome. Low functioning autism, high functioning autism, mild autism, severe autism. The autism spectrum. On the spectrum. Autism spectrum disorder. Disorder, syndrome, condition, red flags, deficits.

Is it any wonder families are confused and disconnected?

From the beginning, families are fed a doom and gloom

narrative, told to immediately engage with "early intervention." These interventions are built upon a generic framework associated with the word autism, deeply rooted in behaviorism and delivered by occupational therapists, speech pathologists, and psychologists. Behaviorism urges a focus onto the autistic child's outer expression.

The child's communication—the byproduct of a rich inner world filled with beauty and intricate, overlapping sensory experiences—those experiences are not of interest to the early intervener. This communication or autistic expression is of no interest to the professional.

The plan for their therapy, their intervention, is shaped and fashioned by neuro-normative standards. Their speech and intonation, the way they move their bodies, the depth and range of their emotional life, and how it is expressed. Our children are put into a semblance of "school of neurotypical etiquette."

"A small window of opportunity" is spouted to families as a sense of panic to encourage us to run toward that window, to intervene, as though our children will remain children, incapacitated for all of their lives.

In the professionals we trust.

When I intuitively identified that my baby was autistic, I was ushered away.

"She's fine."

"No, she wouldn't be smiling if she was autistic."

"Turn off the television for six months and come back and she'll be fine."

"Use your educational expertise and put together an intervention program for her."

I felt completely disempowered, disconnected, and out of my league. I tried everything. I took on the responsibility myself and even trained as a behavioral therapist. The strain and stress of believing my child was so far removed from any human experience I could ever understand was traumatic.

Like many families, we leaned into the intervention that teaches our autistic children to be followers—that dissects their facial expressions and their intonation, their choice of color and thread to wrap around their delightful little selves. The further we immersed ourselves with intervention, the more disconnected we became as a family.

We remortgaged our home and plunged ourselves willingly, yet naively, into debt. All to pay for intervention. I googled and read and watched daytime television on autism. I adopted the narratives of broken marriages and sunk into powerlessness as I watched my child struggle and struggle, with no clue how to help.

I sat inside parent support groups for those who were raising autistic children, only to be engulfed with the heaviness of other people's grief and disappointment in their lives and, sadly, with the children they created. Professionals, educators stood in autism-specific daycares and playgroups, telling parents that they must grieve. They must grieve the loss of the imaginary child they didn't and will never have.

I visited and hid myself in communities laced with parents looking for reasons. Vaccines, adverse reactions to medications, toxic air being breathed in during their pregnancies, fluoride in their water, and chemicals in their packaged foods. The lengths people would go to. The lengths.

There before me was my beautiful baby, her chubby little hands and feet, her spikey hair, and her big brown eyes. So joyous, so lovely. All I wanted to do was love her and enjoy her, and all I was encouraged to do was to be her therapist. Every moment was an opportunity for therapy.

The approaches encouraged by the support on offer to us as a family eventually landed me in bed, chronically ill and burnt out.

One afternoon, after trying to figure out how to continue paying for our child's therapy at $1300 per week, I had a wild idea that I might research what autistic adults actually felt about that same therapy.

I was devastated by what I found.

Significant, intergenerational, prolonged trauma and post-traumatic stress. Autistic children, groomed for predators via the therapeutic approach to turn their No to a Yes.

Within five minutes, I withdrew my child from all therapies.

It was now just her and I, the floor, and some toys. I began to play with her, letting go of the need to turn every moment of connection with her into therapy. It was the first time in months I'd seen my beautiful child smile, laugh, put her arms up for me, and snuggle into me.

I was scared. I had so much unraveling to do. I was sad. I had been lied to. Families everywhere, lied to. The diagnosis of autism is fraught with urgency, alarm, and grief.

Inside of the undoing, the unraveling, the unlearning, was the transformation for our entire family as, one by one, we were all identified and "diagnosed" autistic. For the first time in our lives, we all felt normal.

CHAPTER THREE

The Indoctrination of an Autism Mom

—— MEGHAN ——

S ince this book is about sharing perspectives, I want to start with my own and address the place of privilege from which I come. I'm a white, educated, middle-class woman. I'm well-versed in developmentally appropriate practices, as well as social and emotional learning. I taught elementary school for six years. My mother was the founder and director of a progressively inclusive childcare organization and she helped develop the early intervention program in our state. I attended her daycare as a toddler, volunteered as a preteen, and worked there as a young adult. Early childhood development runs through my veins like that first shot of tequila at a winter solstice bonfire.

When my twins were born prematurely, they received early intervention services immediately following their homecoming from the Neonatal Intensive Care Unit (NICU)—both speech and occupational therapies. Because of their complicated medical histories, our children bypassed the standard 18-month-long waiting list other children had to join in order to get a single pediatric developmental assessment. We had continuous access to the top developmental pediatricians in our area. These doctors knew my children, followed their progress, and gave me continuous feedback. In short, we had access to the best.

I officially left my teaching job when the twins were six

months old so I could focus on their emotional health. I was already on maternity leave and had extended that leave several times due to more hospitalizations. This was a chaotic time for our family, and I also needed to concentrate on the wellbeing of my older children. While my decision to stay home created some financial hardship for our family, our parents stepped in to support us, and they still do to this day.

There are two reasons I'm starting this portion of the book by highlighting my privilege. The first is because I realize that the opportunities given to me aren't afforded to everyone. Many parents are struggling to juggle their work and family lives. Some are working multiple jobs just to stay in their homes. They may not have the time or the wherewithal to research autism or neurodiversity. The majority of parents don't have the educational background to ask questions relevant to childhood development, nor are they able to critically challenge the answers they receive. And unless they work with children in a developmentally appropriate environment, parents may not be knowledgeable about best practices and social and emotional health.

The second reason I'm addressing my privilege is because when it came to my knowledge of autism and how to support my children, *none of that privilege mattered*. Throughout our time in early intervention—attending therapy sessions, evaluations, follow-ups, case management appointments—autism was the one word nobody wanted to mention. Psychologists brought up posttraumatic stress disorder (PTSD) from their trauma in the NICU. Pediatric specialists proposed they had developmental delays due to prematurity. Therapists diagnosed them with receptive and expressive language disorders. Looking back, it was as if they would suggest anything but the A-Word.

In my mind, autism was the mysterious disorder that made that mom want to drive off a bridge with her child in the car (Autism Speaks 2006). It was that scary condition from the other commercial that would steal the joy from our home and break apart our marriage if we... I can't remember exactly how we were supposed to stop that from happening (Autism Speaks 2009).

My misgivings about autism were only magnified by the professionals who worked with my children and their insistence on not bringing it up.

Aside from autism being such a taboo topic, my children's personalities didn't fit the narrow autism-y description I had in my head. Yes, they rocked constantly, but they weren't despondent. They enjoyed rocking together and giggled with each other like it was a game. Sure they had anxiety when we left the house, but they never covered their ears with loud noises. They didn't line up their toys, spin in circles, or fuss about the tags in their shirts. The twins were too engaged with their environment to have an illness so bleak.

By the time they turned two, the twins still didn't speak any mouth words. They cried and screamed to tell us what they wanted. I was concerned about the continuous rocking. And as they got bigger their constant pacing, running, slamming, and furniture destroying became unnerving. Our occupational therapist at the time, who I greatly respected for her knowledge of child development, suggested we ask about sensory processing disorder (SPD).

The doctor we saw was one of the head developmental pediatricians in the area. (I'll call him TopDoc for short.) He immediately shut me down, insisting that SPD was pseudoscience. He brushed their behavior off as something we all do, like when we shake our legs when we're sitting. It wasn't until the twins' three-year check-up that TopDoc casually suggested that one of them be assessed for autism. Nick was saying a few words by then so he wasn't concerned about him. But since Jay still wasn't talking, "We might as well schedule the test."

The Flipping of the Script

When I took Jay to his assessment, the specialist asked me to stay in the waiting room because she didn't want me to interfere with his responses. For the life of me, I'll never understand the logic behind that policy. It seems to me that a screaming child would interfere with results way more than a parent sitting in the corner to provide comfort when needed. I assured her I would be on my best behavior and she reluctantly agreed to let me come back. She used the Autism Diagnostic Observation Schedule (ADOS). It's a play-based assessment with lots of activities and toys, including a creepy bunny that belongs in a horror movie.

I learned more about Jay during that two-hour appointment than I had in the entire previous year. (*The following sentences consist of outdated medical advice that isn't true, but I didn't know it at the time. The specialist performing the assessment offered these insights.*) As I mentioned in Chapter One, she said that he didn't feed the baby doll during the assessment because he didn't care about the happiness of others. (*We purchased his first baby doll the next week so he'd know what to do with it next time.*) I learned that the reason Jay used my arm to point to items he wanted was because he viewed me as a tool or an inanimate object, and not as a real human. (*This is another unfortunate theory from Simon Baron-Cohen.*) She also told me that he had "avoidant behavior," but not to worry. Therapy could correct that.

How could it be that I missed all of this? Was I in denial about who Jay was? The person performing the assessment acted like it was obvious to her and that the information she was giving me was common knowledge. I didn't feel comfortable asking follow-up questions during this interaction. She didn't want me in there to start with, and I definitely didn't want her to kick me out. I was completely bewildered about what she said, and I immediately doubted my confidence in all of the things I thought I knew.

A few weeks later, we followed up with TopDoc for his official findings. He was cool as a cucumber throughout the entire meeting—with a sprinkle of arrogance on top.

"Welp, he has autism." He flashed me the data sheet which I couldn't possibly understand without a couple of hours to study. Even with my educational background, there was too much information to process even a fraction of it.

"His scores indicate Level 3, but I'm gonna diagnose him as Level 2 since he gets along so well. Here's some information for you." He handed me a folder.

"The standard treatment is ABA (applied behavioral analysis). I put a script and a list of providers in the folder. You'll want to get started right away." For the record, those were basically the only things he put in that folder, aside from a useless single-page printout about what autism is.

Gulp!

It's not that I wasn't expecting the diagnosis—I figured he'd qualify due to the comments the examiner made. It was the change in tone and treatment plan that made my heart race. It was as if last week we were supporting his recovery from trauma in the NICU, but now we needed to hurry up and fix him before it was too late.

I knew very little about ABA. But from what I did know, I wasn't a fan. As an advocate for developmentally appropriate practices (NAEYC 2020b), ABA went against everything I believed in. I believed that play was the work of a child and that all learning should be child-led. I believed in the whole language approach to communication—meaning sign language, gestures, and pictures were just as important as speech. I believed that forcing a child to sit at the table to work was absolutely wrong, no matter what.

But now that my child had autism, maybe those principles didn't apply to him? Maybe best practices don't actually work for children who have autism? There must be a reason nobody wanted to mention it before. The twins had over a dozen diagnoses by that time, and nobody tiptoed around any of those. One key difference I noticed was that all of his previous diagnoses offered hope of progress and came with a detailed plan for them to *catch up* by the time they reached elementary school. This diagnosis did not.

And what about Nick? How did he fit into all of this? How was it possible that his identical twin had autism but he didn't? I pressured TopDoc about that but he pushed back, highlighting the differences between the twins. Sure they both rocked and walked on their toes, but Nick started talking a few months prior, and he looked people in the eyes. He was much more social than Jay and had far better motor coordination, "so he clearly doesn't have autism."

Even with all my education, I couldn't formulate educated responses to his answers. He was the authority on this topic with years of schooling and decades of experience, and he was so confident. I was just a mother sitting in the small chair of his exam room, and all I had was a feeling that something didn't add up. I kept reminding myself that we were lucky to be in his office at all, while countless other families remained on the waiting list.

The Autism Mom Factory

Immediately after typing the words *What is autism?* on my computer, I had an advertisement infestation on my computer. Seriously, it was like nothing I'd seen before. Autism Awareness gear covered with puzzle pieces filled my Facebook news feed, while ABA pop-ups interrupted every article I clicked. It was like a whole world I never knew existed, an entire market designed just for parents of children with an autism diagnosis. Shirts, hats, shoes, keychains, phone cases—you name it, there was an autism company selling it! I'll elaborate on this topic further in Chapter Seven.

This was the first time I saw the phrase *Autism Mom*. I probably did see it before then, but I never paid attention. I remember thinking to myself, *Why is this a thing? Are people really doing this? Are parents actually putting their kid's diagnosis on their shirts?* I knew there was a lot of awareness merchandise out there for diseases like cancer and heart conditions, but autism wasn't life threatening. I admit the phrase *Autism Mom* sounded catchy—like that soccer mom bumper sticker on all the SUVs in my neighborhood—but this felt uneasily different.

It's not that I wanted to hide the fact that my child had

autism. Of course I was happy to be his mom. Why wouldn't I be? But if I were going to wear a shirt to celebrate him, putting *his* medical diagnosis with *my* picture seemed like an odd thing to do. I almost felt guilty for *not* buying something—like if I didn't wear the puzzle-piece shirt or display the bumper sticker, I was doing something wrong, or that I must be ashamed of him.

Honestly if it weren't for my other children, I might've ordered some of that swag. By that time, I was a somewhat seasoned mother who chucked that perfect parenting dream in the trash where it belonged a decade prior. My husband and I had three older children from previous relationships who were all in middle school by this time. One of them had a complicated medical history of his own. He was hospitalized multiple times for asthma, pneumonia, and food allergies growing up, and we were still managing his symptoms at the time. Never once did I wear a shirt displaying his medical diagnoses or call myself an *Asthma Mom*, so the thought of doing that for my child who had autism struck me as an odd thing to do.

This Is Why You Make the Big Bucks?

I needed to know everything about autism in order to help Jay progress. Questions swirled through my mind all the time and nothing was adding up. *So what, yesterday he didn't have autism and now he does? And now that he has autism, should we no longer use best practices or be concerned about his emotional development? Why not? Is this because he didn't feed the baby doll?* I was discouraged to see resources I trusted for reliable information, such as the National Institutes of Health advising that children as young as two years old needed intensive intervention. This was in direct contradiction to developmentally appropriate practices for *all* children, no matter what.

I continued my nonstop Google research marathon right up until our next regularly scheduled follow-up appointment about a month later. I was determined to get a better understanding of what autism really was so I could ask TopDoc better questions. The articles I pulled up ranged from genetic to environmental causes, from gut health to my health when I was pregnant. (*I did sneeze that one time…*) There was research on pesticides, gluten, vaccines, nutrient absorption, and processed food. It all seemed a bit suspicious, so I made sure to only click on articles written by doctors associated with prominent hospitals. I gathered up what I thought were the most relevant articles about Jay and his development and went into our appointment ready to learn.

I began by asking TopDoc about apraxia and dyspraxia; both are conditions that involve motor planning (Tziavaras and Sarantopoulos 2020; Reyes 2021). I handed him a few articles I had printed out. Jay obviously had coordination issues and I wondered why we hadn't explored this avenue yet. TopDoc looked at me with a patronizing smirk mixed with a hint of pity, as if he thought it was precious that I went to the Google-y site all by myself…

"It's just autism." He shrugged his shoulders.

He gave the same response when I asked about the other information I came across—the evidence of heavy metal poisoning, yeast overgrowth, and parasites hiding in children's bodies. I felt silly asking because he already shot me down once, and apraxia seemed much more realistic than these other things. I never believed vaccines caused autism. But this was new territory, and I wanted to ensure we weren't missing something.

"Are those conditions we should at least check?"

"No."

That was his entire response, but this time he added a short laugh to his condescending facial expression. It was as if nothing could help my child progress because we had reached the end of the line—the autism trash can in which all other suggestions would get tossed. Apraxia and all of the other things I suggested from my Google search was just a part of autism, and the only treatment he recommended was ABA. Full stop.

A New Community

TopDoc had all but abandoned us. He acted as though my questions were so outlandish that they didn't deserve more than a single word. We were left to fend for ourselves when it came to supporting Jay, and that just wasn't okay with me. I reached out in my favorite international Facebook group for mothers of twins, and a woman in England directed me to an organization here in the United States called the Autism Society. She said she heard it was a great place for parents to connect with other local families. (*That's right. Our doctor didn't even direct us to basic local resources. You really can't make this shit up.*)

As it turned out, our area had a huge community of families! I attended my first local support group meeting that summer. Damn, those ladies (and a couple guys) were *on it*! They made sure I was signed up for services and walked me through applying for those we didn't yet have. They knew assessment workers and school personnel by their first names and gave me the inside scoop on the twins' new principal. They referred me to a brand new doctor who they all used, and promised to put in a good word for me since his waiting list was over a year long. That evening was the first time I didn't feel helpless and alone. I finally had a community I could call on to answer my questions without worrying that I would get shut down.

After that first meeting, the Autism Society crew invited me to another local parenting group. Spectrum Parents had an active Facebook group and hosted events that were accessible to my children. They rented out indoor trampoline parks, held private ice-skating events, and got together at the beach. They even partnered with other organizations in the community and my kids joined a pressure-free running club. When I needed something, they were there to help. When I wanted to get out of the house, they always welcomed my family. When my kids started running in opposite directions, they helped me keep them safe. Never once did they judge me or tell me to get control of my kids. It was an amazing feeling to find a community of parents who *got it*.

Round Two

At the encouragement of my new friends, I insisted that Nick get tested for autism as soon as possible. His appointment was scheduled soon after with the head child psychologist in the developmental pediatrics practice. As far as doctor hierarchies go, there was no professional more qualified to assess him. She was as exclusive as they come. The discrepancy between Jay and Nick's diagnosis was the most confusing part about autism to me, and we were finally going to get the answers we were looking for. Or so we thought.

"Well, you were looking for answers and this is it," she said matter-of-factly. She went on to inform us that Nick showed no signs of autism; however, his IQ score was in the 50s. *I knew the score couldn't possibly be accurate. And what are the odds that his identical twin had autism, and he had something completely different?*

"So the rocking, toe walking, and anxiety aren't signs?"

"He's way too social to have autism. He gives fairly good eye contact, and he seeks out approval from adults. Children with autism just don't do that."

Her assessment sounded eerily familiar, but we had no choice but to go with the results. If anyone would know about autism, it was her. I was devastated for weeks after our appointment. We were sure that we'd leave with a better understanding than we came in with, but instead we only ended up with more questions.

CHAPTER FOUR

What a Relief!

— JULES —

As a child, I was an eloper, mess-maker, nudist with sensory difficulties. I had an affinity for water and stair cartwheels, and an inability to pronounce even my own name. My family jokingly gave me two Indian names—"Little Naked Running Girl" and "Crash Boom Bang Fall Down the Stairs."

Today, I'm a late-diagnosed autistic and ADHD mother of three Black and Ojibwe autistic children, one diagnosed at each pseudo "level" of autism. I am a community builder. I've been the first person that people have asked, "Am I autistic?" I've been the first person that parents of autistic children have asked, "What do I do?" I am a complex and whole human being. I am autistic, and I'm not missing a piece.

Parenting is the most important, most difficult, and most rewarding thing I've ever done in my life, and I'm doing it alone. As a young solo parent with a family that isn't close or particularly supportive, I did not have the support system that is recommended to all parents by parenting books and professionals alike. I sought parenting support, but typical parent support groups didn't really understand our circumstances. Whether in-person or online, I couldn't relate to other parents, and they couldn't relate to me.

"Enroll him in karate so he'll learn some self-discipline," and "Send him to me for the summer, I'll straighten him out," are a couple of the more common suggestions I would get from parents of neurotypical kids who just didn't get it. It was useless advice, and I felt so isolated because no one seemed to understand us. A lot of parents of autistic children feel like this, and it's amplified for autistic parents of autistic kids.

Tyler, my eldest, is now an adult. He's a bit of an introvert with the kindest heart of anyone I've ever met. When he smiles, my heart soars. He fit the flappy, little professor stereotype when he was younger, happy to infodump about Pokemon and the electric grid. These days his primary interest is video games, and he's still developing a direction and plans for his future. He's mentioned welding and disability support as potential paths, but he's hesitant to interact with people he doesn't know because he's experienced intense bullying from allistic (non-autistic) people. In the meantime, he's home and being supported on his own terms.

Johnathan, my second-born child, is a teen who loves music and anime. He spoke late and we relied on baby sign language and simple gestures to communicate until he was ready to use mouth words. When away from home, Tyler spoke to others to communicate on Johnathan's behalf, although this dynamic has flipped since they've gotten older. In younger years, he was a twinkly eyed mischievous charmer who negotiated everything from chores to dinner, and never stopped moving. Today, adults comment on how polite and welcoming he is to others. He is intrinsically motivated and tasks that he doesn't choose to do simply aren't done. Throughout the Covid-19 pandemic, he learned how to speak Japanese so he could watch Naruto in its original language, and he's learned how to professionally produce and record music.

My youngest child, River, is elementary school aged. She's a cheeky and determined child who's passionate about dogs and Roblox. She rejects all forms of direct instruction, so we parallel learn and I sneak unconventional education into our daily home-school life. When she's stressed, she is a wolf who hides in a wolf den, and other people don't generally know how to deal with that. She's inquisitive and loves connecting with people on her own terms. She's a sensitive soul who loves love and hates hate.

As a parent, I recognize my responsibility to cultivate the best part of my children and guide them into adulthood prepared to live good lives. I joke that my children are feral, but I've found that when they are able to make decisions for themselves, with support and guidance, they are happiest and most successful. I'm a different parent for each of my children. We each have different relationships, and those relationships have changed as my children have grown. They need different things from me, and I take seriously my responsibility to become the parent they need, while recognizing I haven't always been the parent they needed. I feel so much gratitude that I get to be their parent, and so much regret for all of the times I got it wrong.

In Ojibwe, we learn that our children choose us to be their parents before they are born. They choose us because they believe that we can become the parent that they need us to be. Here I am, an ordinary and pitiful person, tasked with raising, teaching, and guiding tiny humans into adulthood. They chose me to take on this enormous responsibility. In our parenting journeys, we are meant to grow as much as our children do.

This teaching has been misinterpreted by some to blame children for choosing bad parents, which is a colonized and entitled way to shirk responsibility for parental growth. If anything, this teaching makes parenting even more of a sacred responsibility. Believing that adulthood makes us better than our children, that we know all of the answers and they should always obey, is arrogance and greed.

Introduction to Autism

I didn't know I was autistic, I didn't know my children were autistic, I just knew that life was complicated and difficult for no apparent reason. We needed help, and no meaningful help was available. I was impatient, frustrated, and cried and yelled a lot. I was neither the parent I wanted to be nor the parent my children needed. Had I had accurate and helpful information early on, my family wouldn't have suffered with lack of meaningful support.

I didn't have useful information, and I was not able to be the parent my children needed, although I certainly tried.

I was searching for answers about our struggles, and autism was in the periphery. I knew it existed. It had even been suggested in passing by my sons' elementary school, but it was only suggested in retaliation when I made a complaint about how my children were being bullied and treated unfairly—not introduced as a resource. When I asked questions about the school's evaluation process, they refused to answer questions and excluded me. I couldn't proceed without a full understanding of what they were evaluating, how they were evaluating, and what the next steps after evaluation would be.

I had even reviewed the diagnostic criteria for autism. But the language wasn't language that made sense to me. The words they used, "deficit" and "highly restricted" and "abnormal," were so unkind that I couldn't apply them to my children. Descriptions like "simple motor stereotypies" and "hyper- or hyporeactivity to sensory input" didn't even make sense to me. There needed to be some kind of plain language and non-stigmatizing way to describe autism, because not every parent sees their child as a sum of their deficits.

I couldn't accept autism as a diagnosis until I understood it. I knew something was different about my children, but I didn't know what it was. I clung to the idea of "asynchronous development." My children were brilliant, capable, friendly, talkative, loving, funny. All things that I wrongly believed were incompatible with an autism diagnosis because I was taught that autism is bad and wrong and burdensome, and children with autism couldn't possibly be connected to their parents. After all, autistic people lived in their own world.

I love, appreciate, and celebrate my children, and that was incompatible with what I'd been taught about autism. I understood them because they were like me. They were *so* much like me. Smart, but had a hard time with homework. Friendly, but struggled socially and experienced bullying. Talkative, but said the wrong thing. Funny, but inappropriate.

Was I experiencing denial about autism? Perhaps, though I knew there was something going on. My skepticism was more of an instinctive refusal of the idea that the construct of autism as a tragedy could ever fit into our lives. My children are gifts, not burdens. Even on the most difficult days, I felt that I was the one failing, never them.

One morning while at work, I was chatting with Angela, a colleague and friend, about my frustrations with my son's school. I was upset with the difficulty in getting the school staff to understand and work with my child. Johnathan had 169 pages of behavioral referrals in the first and second grade alone. The school picked on him over petty things. They weren't choosing their battles, they wanted him to comply with directives without understanding them, they wanted him to sit still and look at the board, they wanted him to *not* have a Lego guy in his pocket to fidget with, they wanted him to do all kinds of things he just couldn't do.

Angela, a parent of an autistic child, looked me in the eyes, which was rare for her, and said, "As long as he's not autistic, right?" She turned around, walked to her desk, and went to work without another word.

That moment was pivotal for me. My cheeks burned. She had patiently listened to me be an ableist jerk about autism for months. And it hadn't even occurred to me that I was being insulting. I didn't know any better. I hadn't thought of it that way. I never would have said anything mean about her son. He's a great kid, even though he happened to have autism. But I was perpetuating the message that I'd learned: autism is bad and it is to be avoided at all costs. I understood autism to be an accessory to a person, an add-on, if you will. Lovable people sometimes have autism, but the autism is a hardship that needs to be corrected.

"I don't want him to use it as an excuse," I said to someone suggesting an evaluation, rejecting that he needed support.

"My child is not disabled!" I protested to a special education teacher, offended that anyone would say that my child is unable to do whatever he wants to do.

"But he's so smart," I protested. In this statement I perpetuated ableism against people with intellectual disabilities, and invalidated autistic people who don't have co-occurring intellectual disability in one fell swoop—cementing the fact that I did not know a single thing about what autism actually is. The only thing that I knew about autism was the information offered by the white parents, white researchers, and white medical providers who had the financial and social capital to market autism to the public.

At the same time, as an unidentified autistic adult, I was dealing with major issues that autistic adults commonly face—domestic violence, sexual assault, job instability, income insecurity, burnout, lack of social support, and homelessness. I was left wondering why life was so damn difficult, and why no one else seemed to be struggling the way I was. I needed support, and I couldn't get it. Meanwhile, my children needed support and I was the barrier.

Identification

When I finally learned more about autism and realized it was time to pursue evaluations for my children, I wasn't prepared for the systemic racism and sexism that we would experience. Autism as a diagnosis exists based on research of young white boys from affluent and well-connected families. There are enormous disparities in identifying autistic people of color and autistic girls and nonbinary people (CDC 2020).

Tyler was fairly easily diagnosed. He fit many of the stereotypes that were based on the research of young, white boys: flappy, avoided eye contact, recited monologs about topics he was passionate about, and had a hard time connecting with other kids.

The clinic initially refused to even evaluate Johnathan for autism during his team neuropsychology evaluation. They'd already diagnosed him with oppositional defiant disorder (ODD), attention deficit hyperactivity disorder (ADHD), and neurodevelopmental disorder–unspecified. ODD didn't seem accurate to me. Over months of learning with the intensity of an autistic with a special interest, I could give examples of all of the ways that autism, particularly a pathological demand avoidance (PDA) profile, was a more accurate explanation for what his teachers and I were noticing. During the appointment to review his evaluation, I described how I believed their results supported an autism diagnosis. They begrudgingly added an autism specialist to the team, and the autism specialist later confirmed my hunch. His autism diagnosis was added to his neuropsychological evaluation as an aside.

Who Has the Map?

When my children were diagnosed, I was given copies of their diagnostic assessments and sent on my way. I was frustrated by this at first. The doctors gave me a confirmation of this diagnosis that I suspected, but that was it. No flow chart, no road map, no useful information about how to help them. Someone later told me this is referred to as the "diagnose and dump" experience. I felt lost because I thought there would be someone to help me figure out what to do.

In my quest to learn what I should do next, I found local social media groups for "autism parents" and general groups for autistic people. I joined several of them, thinking I would find people who would understand the dynamics, strengths, and challenges that my family was experiencing. What I actually found was a divided community, and I felt even more lost. It's so easy for people to get sucked into a compartment of belonging, and their beliefs are then shaped and formed by the groups of people that they first encounter and feel supported by. I just wanted to feel a sense of belonging, because so far, life and parenting had felt so desperately lonely.

There is no roadmap or flow chart or manual about how to parent autistic kids, because every child is different and needs different things. Parents are caught in between decades of misinformation and conflict, trying to do what they think is right for their children. I believe that most parents want what is best for their children, even if they are misguided, or don't know how, or if they are ill equipped or unsupported. Many parents harboring ableism love their children and want what's best for them—even if we have different understandings of what "best" means.

In my frustration and feelings of overwhelm, I decided to take an AutismMoon. I'll discuss this in more detail later in the book. Instead of hastily moving forward with therapies, I took time to learn without committing to anything in particular, the only goal being learning from a variety of perspectives. Today, I'm thankful for this time of exploration because I was given the freedom to explore what autism meant for my children and my family as a whole. Learning about autism within the context of my culture was an important part of understanding my role as a parent.

Wait a Minute... Me Too!

Once I realized that my eldest child was autistic, I needed to know why.

Was it because I had been forced to take Pitocin while in labor?

Was it because I struggled to breastfeed, and I had to supplement with formula?

Was it vaccines?

Was it because I gave him acetaminophen after his vaccines?

Was it the febrile seizure?

Was it exposure to toxins in his environment?

Was it lead?

It took some time to find the cause of my children's autism. Genetics. Specifically, heritable genetics. During my own

AutismMoon, I kept finding myself in the information I was exploring. I began to recognize autistic traits in myself, and evaluating my life with this new lens of understanding autism, it seemed like a reasonable explanation.

When I learned about stimming, I thought it was just a funny coincidence that the silly thing that I have done with my fingers since elementary school was a combination of echolalia and stimming. I get a word or phrase stuck in my head, and I type it out on my fingers, over and over and over. It was both an attempt to stay alert and process information that I was taking in. The therapist that I saw throughout high school thought it was notable and he'd ask what I was typing any time he noticed it.

I don't know if he ever considered autism as a possibility, but he never mentioned it. The more pressing issue at the time was that I couldn't stay awake. I slept at night, but still fell asleep at times that I didn't want or mean to fall asleep. That's when I collected my first diagnosis: narcolepsy. Treatment? Ritalin. And stimming, because stimming helped me stay awake. If I kept moving, it was less likely that I would need to curl up into a ball under the table in class and take a nap. When I stopped moving, I slept, whether I wanted to or not.

In my early 20s, I sought a new therapist which resulted in a diagnosis of ADHD and PTSD. During the intake process, they asked why I was seeking therapy, and I answered, "Everyone thinks I'm a bitch." I experienced social and communication difficulties my entire life. In early adulthood, my roommates nicknamed me the "Ice Queen" because I wasn't as warm or sociable as women are expected to be. My so-called flat affect or resting-bitch-face made me seem unapproachable to others, and on the rare occasion that I made a friend, they would tell me, "I thought you were a bitch until I got to know you." This is not the compliment that people think it is. None of those comments felt good, and I internalized all of these messages into believing that I was just plain unlikeable.

I have frequent miscommunications with people, often getting stuck on one small part of a conversation and being unable to move on until the miscommunication was cleared up. It led to a lot of conflict, and it was conflict that I wasn't choosing, and also couldn't disengage from. Somehow, when there's a conflict between an allistic person and an autistic person, the autistic person is blamed. Whether we're accused of being too direct or not direct enough, or accused of lacking empathy, we are always to blame. Because autism is perceived to be wrong, every time.

I couldn't keep up with the demands of everyday life. I was working, attending night school, trying to raise children by myself, and volunteering. I was burnt out, but if I stopped, then I couldn't do anything. I needed to be fully engaged, always busy with a full and strict schedule and routine, with lots of projects, or else I was a potato. There was no in-between. I couldn't recognize my limitations, and I pushed myself too hard because capitalism trained me to believe that if I was taking a break, then I was worthless, and there was no safety net when I needed a break. Taking a break resulted in homelessness. That was the ever-present threat. This level of stress led to being an impatient and angry parent, something my children didn't deserve.

I found a list of autistic traits and experiences that are common for women, and it took me by surprise because I could check so many of the boxes. I found research papers listing common co-occurring conditions, like lazy eye, which I'd been bullied mercilessly for as a child and had corrected as an adult. I found documents describing the history of autism and raised my eyebrows to learn that my biological father's diagnosis of childhood schizophrenia was how they labeled autism in those days. I found a note in a journal article about being hyposensitive to cold and hypersensitive to heat as examples of sensory processing difficulties. I read the article "'I Thought I Was Lazy': The Invisible Day-to-Day Struggle for Autistic Women" by Reese Piper (2017) and then, I knew.

Once again, I picked up the phone to request an evaluation. The third clinic I called was willing to complete an autism evaluation, and after several months, and hours of completing unbearable forms while rolling around on the floor of a clinic a few months later, I had my diagnosis. Filling out forms while sitting in chairs at tables is a thing I can't do.

Learning the language of autism is what helped me recognize my own identity.

I Cried at "Severe"

River was evaluated for autism when she was 4. Because of my new understanding of autism, I noticed patterns that fit the diagnosis. I naively thought that having an early and accurate diagnosis would enhance her school experience.

"Her test scores indicate autism, but we're going to diagnose ADHD and anxiety." The assessor smiled as she told me what she thought was good news.

"She knows you like coffee," the assessor explained as an example of why she couldn't possibly be autistic. I was annoyed. Everyone who has ever met me knows that I like coffee. I have narcolepsy. I've been reliant on coffee to stay awake and alert for every day of my life since I was a teen. What about her inability to speak? What about her difficulties with transitions? What about her sensory sensitivities? What about her impulsivity? What about her desperate reactions to distress? What about elopement?

I sought a second evaluation because by this time I knew that, as a young Black and Indigenous girl, the likelihood of her getting an accurate diagnosis was low. This time, we went to a smaller clinic. We provided copies of her initial evaluation, and the new assessor reviewed her records and completed some additional evaluations.

When her second diagnostic assessment came in the mail, I held onto it for a few hours before opening. I read it, somewhat surprised by the results and disturbed by the pathologizing language. Severe. Low adaptive functioning. Predictions of poor outcomes and inability to do things. I cried.

I didn't cry because she's autistic, I cried because I didn't want her to struggle the way that I have. I love who she is, completely, and there's nothing about her that I would change. I would, however, remove the barriers that she will face in her lifetime in a heartbeat. I would remove the risks of harm. Life isn't easy for autistic people, and especially not for autistic girls of color. I took her diagnosis so hard because I wanted her to live a safer and happier life than I have lived.

Due to her age and that nasty "severe" word in her evaluation, early intensive behavioral intervention and applied behavior analysis were suggested as treatments. Thankfully, because of the time I'd spent learning before her diagnosis, I knew that neither were options for us. But had I not already researched, would I have gone down that path? When my sons were diagnosed, I hoped that someone would tell me what to do. If I didn't already have information about the harms of behaviorism, I would have been thankful for the suggestions.

I love my children, and I want to do what is right for them, and behaviorism is the first and most frequent recommendation for autistic children. I only knew what was right for my children by listening to people with lived experience, and by learning about autism with an open heart. My only goal was to do right by my children, whatever that meant.

Key Points

- Confusion is common for parents of newly diagnosed autistic children. This is due to the misinformation parents receive—throughout our lives and at the time of diagnosis.

- Parents commonly recognize autistic traits within themselves after their children are identified. Explore books and resources created by autistic adults to learn more.

- Doctors are not always correct. Parents should trust themselves, and challenge information that doesn't seem right. Don't be afraid to find another provider.

- Autistic children would benefit from parents taking time after their children's autism diagnosis, before committing to any therapies or interventions. Be sure to get a variety of perspectives, as the autistic community is not a monolith.

Resources to Explore

"100-ish Books on Autism and Neurodiversity"

https://notanautismmom.com/2020/07/20/autism-books

"'I Thought I Was Lazy': The Invisible Day-to-Day Struggle for Autistic Women" by Reese Piper

https://medium.com/the-establishment/i-thought-i-was-lazy-the-invisible-day-to-day-struggle-for-autistic-women-6268515175f3

"A Guide to Understanding Your Autistic Child" by Autistic Science Person

https://autisticscienceperson.com/2021/01/05/a-guide-to-understanding-your-autistic-child

THE WORST OF
EACH OTHER

Kieran Rose

When we talk about a division that exists between autistic advocates and parents of autistic children, we need to be careful in how we conceptualize that division and importantly identify what actually creates that division.

Despite social media platforms often being filled with what is perceived as tension, bickering, and name calling, we're not actually looking at two groups which are diametrically opposed, with different goals and objectives. These are two groups that mostly share the same aims and have the same vested interests. They both want change, they both want autistic people to be supported; and both groups are traumatized in different ways by the narratives around autistic people.

Both groups are coming at the same objectives but unfortunately from different directions and with different levels of understanding. From a parental viewpoint—indeed from the viewpoint of much of the world—being autistic is a negative thing. It's grounded in deficits, quirks, and abnormalities that all go against the social grain that make an autistic person non-productive in a capitalist-driven world. It's fuelled a narrative that dictates that autism is a childhood "thing," that it is something which is grown out of, that autistic people are child-like and incompetent.

Why?

Because nearly a century ago, two men decided that was so. Two men whose work still underpins everything everyone thinks they know about autism, which is all based on observation and the assumption that because a person doesn't follow social conventions and exists in a wholly different way, there is something wrong with them.

A parent's first introduction to autism in terms of identifying and getting their child diagnosed is usually negative. The diagnostic process is of itself pathologizing and reinforces negativity. The professionals delivering the diagnosis are often medical people, grounded in medicalized language and thought-processes and, frankly, a lot of ableist practice.

This is coupled with the narrative that we are spun about parenthood by society. We are sold "the dream": about girls in pink dresses and boys rolling in the mud, who grow up and go to colleges and universities, who become teachers and doctors and have their beautiful houses with white picket fences, who in turn have their own perfect, model children.

We all visualize and conceptualize our children's futures, the paths laid out in front of them. But the reality of this is not so. What we "hope" for our children as parents is what we are told to "hope" for. We are conditioned socially to socially condition and perpetuate a cycle of social myths based not on reality, but the selling of "the dream."

When we have an autistic child, those hopes and dreams are dashed, either because we are sold the myth that no autistic child can achieve any of that, or the assumption that if they don't have any of that they will not have amounted to anything in their lives. So, we get sucked into a world of normalization, where we're convinced that this therapy and that therapy will "work," that it will make our child "whole" and "fully normal." That we can have the prince or princess that we hoped for.

So, enter an autistic advocate, who on an unconscious level is already undermining "the dream" just by existing, because that autistic advocate is a grown-up fully autistic version of the parent's autistic child. When we have a child it's difficult to imagine them as an adult, particularly as an adult that we really don't want them to turn into, so to be shown that autistic children grow up to be autistic adults who are still just as autistic can be a shock. "The dream" can't happen if your child struggles, "the dream" can't happen if the behavioral therapies designed to fix them doesn't, or social skills training doesn't normalize them.

When that autistic advocate presents information about those therapies, it is often met with disbelief and derision. The deliverance of the reality that those therapies are designed to appeal to our base urges of social conformity, designed to reignite belief that "the dream" is achievable, is too complicated to compute. It conflicts with the negative narrative that the parent has learnt to rely on, sold by doctors and teachers and a thousand autism experts around the world.

With the delivery of this information also comes the perception that how autistic adults communicate is incorrect. An autistic adult might deliver information which isn't wrapped up in fluff and social niceties, which is then perceived as "rudeness" or "aggression" but really means that the person receiving the information both doesn't like that information because it conflicts with their worldview and they don't like how that information is being delivered—because again it reminds them that the person they are talking to is an autistic adult.

That the autistic person may speak or write seems to bring with it a certain amount of confusion which culminates in the strange conclusion that the autistic person isn't autistic "enough," or that somehow this tiny snapshot into their lives is enough to know how that autistic person exists all the time and is representative of the fact that they have never had any struggles at all.

From an autistic person's perspective, the frustration that the parent is unable or unwilling to listen is immense. That and the defensiveness being shown by the parent can then trigger an understandable trauma response which causes both sides to rapidly escalate.

What we are seeing when we look at that division is two things: a gulf in knowledge and a lack of respect of culture.

There is an enormous amount of knowledge within the autistic community. It is knowledge which is driving fundamental change through both activism and research.

Research is now slowly starting to catch up with autistic people in its recognition and understanding of things which autistic people have been discussing for decades: autistic masking and burnout, that communication is generally freer and more effective amongst autistic people, that functioning labels are harmful, that we do in fact often have buckets of empathy and that we don't have extreme male brains.

Also, most importantly, that concepts such as "severe" autism don't exist. That different groups are talking about autism in different ways and mostly as umbrella labels including things that are not autism and ignoring the neurological system which is. That describing us as a homogeneous group, without recognizing both the negative role of co-occurring conditions and the individuality of us all that leaves us connected through strong threads of relatable existence and shared neurological processing, is both damaging and a false economy.

Which is where culture comes in.

The autistic community has the burgeoning beginnings of a unique culture, a culture that until recently was dispersed and isolated, scattered across the world and which has found both online and offline connectivity via the internet. All the markers of a culture are there, in our shared communication and language use, the terminology we have created, the social norms that exist amongst autistic people, the ideas and customs, the development of art and writing framed around autistic experience, the development of technology, the shared patterns of behavior, movement, and thought, and the recognition of collective trauma.

None of this is recognized currently outside of the autistic community, and the insistence of non-autistic people that autistic people exist solely within non-autistic culture is incredibly damaging, especially when we live in a shared world. We keep being told that we must live in the "real" world, which really means we must exist as non-autistic people or be excluded. That the real world also incorporates autistic way of being and autistic culture is never identified.

So, we have not a divide, but a culture gap, one devoid of the correct information. Bridging that gap enables autistic people to have strong allies who are working towards shared objectives from the same direction. It enables parents to have an enormous resource to help support them to enable their children to become beautifully authentic autistic adults, who understand themselves and are able to confidently advocate for themselves.

We bridge that gap by parents recognizing that currently autistic people, a traumatized and marginalized group, are currently doing all the heavy lifting, by autistic people recognizing that parents are traumatized and victimized, just in different ways.

This is happening. I've developed training with a shared community space around it, that autistic people, parents, and professionals keep coming back to again and again. Others have done it by creating shared spaces where the autistic voice is centered and respected, but knowledge is presented in the form of things like book clubs for shared learning, or by the ability to ask questions and respectfully listen to answers, and often leads to parents recognizing their own neurodivergence and trauma.

The more parents understand the concepts discussed here, the weight of research and knowledge that lies behind the neurodiversity paradigm, and what it means to actually be autistic, the better they will be equipped to support their children in ways that encourage them to grow, thrive, and one day become the unicorn that is the non-traumatized autistic person, which is what we all should really be striving for, the real dream.

CHAPTER FIVE

Why Are You Yelling at Me?

— MEGHAN —

My relationship with the autistic community got off to a rocky start. Only a few months after Jay was diagnosed, I started a blog called *Not an Autism Mom*. At the time, I felt overwhelmed and isolated. I had so many questions and very few answers. I used my blog to share my experiences, and hopefully connect with a broader community who could understand what I was going through.

I chose the name *Not an Autism Mom* for a few reasons. First and foremost, I was *beyond* sick of seeing those advertisements on my computer. I swear it was like they were trying to make me join some sort of cult. I could hear this voice late at night under my bed whispering, "We're waiting for you, Meghan. Join us as we crush the autisms..." Not really, but you get my point. It was creepy! As you'll learn in this chapter, I didn't know anything about the autistic community's issues with the phrase *Autism Mom* or the history of its use. It's just a fortunate coincidence that the name fits my viewpoints today.

Honestly, I never wanted my blog to be autism specific. When I first started writing, my articles touched on lots of different subjects. I wrote about parenting twins, my experience in the NICU, raising Black and Brown children in a racist world, and adjusting to the stay-at-home mom life. I even wrote an article about the benefits of owning a Swiss army knife. My life didn't revolve around my kids, in theory at least, so I didn't want to create a website that was only about autism.

One of the first articles I published highlighted the new parenting community I mentioned in my previous chapter. I wrote about how much these parents were teaching me and how thankful I was for their help. At the time, my following was tiny and consisted mostly of friends and family. Imagine my surprise when a complete stranger left this comment:

> If you're not learning from autistic adults, you're not doing it right.

Wait, what? Who was this anonymous person stomping on the one shred of happiness I had to share, telling me what I'm doing wrong? We will fight. After five months of practically *begging* TopDoc to answer my questions, I finally found this amazing community of parents who understood what I was going through. They were helping me navigate services, inviting my family to events, and serenading me with support. Because of them, I no longer felt isolated.

Furthermore, what did that comment even mean? I didn't know there *was* an adult autistic community. I realize how that sounds, but it's true. I'd never heard that phrase before. How could people with autism form a community without being able to talk or think? It didn't make sense to me. It's not that I thought children grew out of it, but TopDoc never mentioned these adults before. He damn sure didn't mention anything about my own child being able to read or write. Temple Grandin was the only autistic adult I knew of who had the ability to talk at conferences, but I figured she was some sort of exception. How was I supposed to learn from a community that didn't actually exist?

How I Met Jules...

Not even a month later, I encountered my co-author Jules for the first time, after writing a different article—this one was out of pure frustration. Following the recommendation of my newfound parenting friends, I applied for one of my state's Medicaid waivers that could offer our family some much needed support. I went through the screening process, filled out the paperwork, and endured the judgmental in-home assessment, only to find out that my children were too young/not disabled enough to qualify for services. I couldn't tell at the time which metric was actually to blame.

I should've known they wouldn't get approved when I first called. The nurse who did the assessments asked me if my kids had any diagnoses. I listed them all and added autism at the end. She stopped me mid-sentence and said, "Well that doesn't mean he'll qualify. Autism is just a behavioral diagnosis." *Yes that's right, the nurse in charge of medical waivers for the entire city thought of autism in that way.* In Chapter Seven, I elaborate on why her statement was woefully inaccurate. We would eventually be denied five times for this service over the next two years.

My world felt like it was crumbling around me with no hope of relief or support, so I used my blog to vent. I titled the post "Autism is Nothing Like Going to Holland—Welcome to the Jungle." It was a parody of "Welcome to Holland" by Emily Perl Kingsley (1987), a poem I had grown to loathe. I wrote about how confused I was as a new parent on this autism journey. I talked about my children's constant screaming and me not being able to understand their cries. I referenced the conflicting information I received from each person I talked to, and how I had no idea it would be this hard to find support.

"Welcome to the Jungle" was my first viral article. I was overwhelmed by the attention it drew. Parents from all over the world seemed to be in the same jungle I was in, and they were just as desperate. As I scrolled through the comment section of my Facebook post, one in particular jumped out at me. It was Jules.

You know, your kids are going to read this one day and they'll feel like a burden because of the words you're writing. (#actuallyautistic)

First of all... No seriously, my head could've popped off from the steam building up in my body. Who was this "actually autistic adult" and what did she know about my kids and our lives? She had the ability to read my article, form an opinion about it, and type her nasty response in my comment section. It must be nice sitting behind her computer attacking parents like me who are just trying to make it through the day. My kids couldn't talk, they didn't seem to understand basic words, hell they couldn't even sit down for five minutes to watch a television show. My walls were filled with holes, my furniture was destroyed, and I hadn't had a good night's rest in over three years. If this lady had autism, it was obviously a different kind. She should mind her business and take her negativity somewhere else.

Thank the Manufacturer I didn't actually type any of that for Jules or the rest of the world to see, but it was in fact exactly how I felt. Instead, I respectfully disagreed with her and justified my article by explaining that not all parenting is sunshine and rainbows. While that particular post wasn't my most loving article, I wrote plenty of others highlighting our good days. Jules wasn't swayed by my explanation, and for the next few months she stuck around my page pointing out my ableism. She didn't, however, teach me a better way or provide me with any resources. All I knew is that she didn't like me, and she made that point perfectly clear.

I found myself at a crossroad with nothing but dead ends in sight. Months had passed since Jay was diagnosed with autism. Nick was diagnosed with something I knew wasn't right, and I was no closer to figuring out how to best support them. TopDoc was useless, I was fighting for services that my children would ultimately never receive, and now an autistic adult was trolling my page, calling me names like *Martyr Mom*, and I didn't even know what that meant!

The Book that Changed My Life
Only a few weeks after meeting Jules, and over half a year since Jay's diagnosis, I learned about a book called *The Reason I Jump*

co-written by Naoki Higashida (Higashida *et al.* 2013), a non-speaking boy in Japan. This was the first time I heard of a child like mine being able to think, process information, reflect, and write a book.

Up until that point, the professionals we saw didn't offer any examples of nonspeaking autistic...well anything. There was a complete void, and I didn't even know the correct words to type into Google. I immediately ordered the book and devoured it in one sitting.

This kid... He blew my mind! Naoki wrote the book in a simple Q&A format, answering basic questions that parents like me would want to know. For example, Why are your sleep patterns messed up? And, Why do you wander off? Naoki answered these questions in detail, with the simplicity and sincerity that only a child could express. He talked about his body and his mind in a way that made sense to me. He didn't use phrases like *sensory input* or *apraxia*. Instead, he referred to his own senses and feelings. I could actually visualize what Naoki was saying and relate it to my own kids.

I mention *The Reason I Jump* in interviews, conferences, and in this book for a few reasons: Firstly, it's a fantastic and accessible book for busy parents who don't have much time to read. Secondly, this book was a turning point for me. It was the missing link in my quest for understanding this confusing condition they called autism. I finally found validation in the uneasy feelings I had from claims the doctors made and found actual answers to the questions they refused to address.

If I'm being completely honest though, the real reason I mention this book is to point out the negligence of every single doctor I encountered until that point. That may sound harsh, but my accusation matches the impact of their actions. I cannot for the life of me understand how doctors are allowed to treat a specific group of patients without learning from and listening to that specific community.

I realize I'm speaking from a privileged position and that disabled people have been saying this for decades, but it's maddening to me that *any* professional working in a developmental pediatric practice wouldn't know about a book written by a nonspeaking autistic boy who gives first-hand testimony about his own experience as an autistic child, and recommend that book to parents. Even now as I'm writing these words four years later, I meet parents every single day who don't realize there are books written by autistic authors. It's as if professionals are actively keeping these primary sources of information from us, and that's not okay.

The Reason I Jump changed my entire learning strategy. From the moment I started reading autistically authored books, I was hooked. I felt confident that I was on the right path to finding the answers I'd been searching for. I joined autistic-led Facebook groups, followed #ActuallyAutistic Twitter accounts, and I invited autistic bloggers to write for my website. The floodgates finally opened, and I was swimming in useful information.

Ummm, Ouch?

As excited as I was to find the autistic community, I felt utterly incompetent entering their space. It was like that time I tested into a high level Spanish class my first year in college and everyone knew what the teacher was saying except for me. These advocates used words and acronyms I didn't understand. They referred to events and information I wasn't familiar with. Even with a background in education and early intervention, it was all a bit overwhelming and I struggled to keep up.

They challenged my use of person-first language (PFL). Their argument in favor of identity-first language (IFL) went against the core values I was brought up with and taught to my own children.

> "Autistic" doesn't define us, but it does describe us. It is an adjective, after all. An adjective which describes a diagnosable condition. Not an insult. Not a slur. Just a word which describes a quality... [W]hen you use person-first language to

refer to someone else, you are marking their illness or disability as negative. And when you do that, you step into dangerous territory. Some people resent the suggestion that the word for their disability is so distasteful that they should hold it at arm's length, like it's a dead fish. (C.L. Lynch 2019)

They challenged my use of functioning levels and mental age, the descriptions that *every single* professional used and *every single* report displayed until that point.

For those labelled high functioning, it can be incredibly difficult to get external support once diagnosed... High functioning is not how an autistic person experiences being autistic. It's how society experiences the autistic person...

While 'high functioning' is used to presume competence, 'low functioning' is often used to deny autonomy... Autistic people in this cohort are often exposed to abusive therapies, such as Applied Behavioural Analysis (ABA), to try to 'normalise' their behaviours. (Williams 2019)

They insisted that these terms in fact infantilized and disrespected my children. A few even used the words *abusive* and *dehumanizing* to describe my language and that of other parents in the groups I'd joined.

Learning about **ableism** took me down an uncomfortable and slightly confrontational path. If you had asked me before entering these autistic-led spaces, I would've sworn up and down that I didn't have an ableist bone in my body. But these autistic adults challenged my views in a way nobody else could. They called me out on using phrases like *diff-ability* and *differently abled*. They suggested that I preferred those phrases because somewhere deep within I viewed disabled people as less-than. They said that using those words was my attempt to make my children seem more valuable, whether I realized it or not (Brown 2021).

The information they offered was in complete contradiction to the information I received from the professionals. Even some of my most basic parenting strategies were deemed harmful.

I remember thinking, there's no way that *everything* I knew was wrong. These strangers couldn't know what they were talking about. Anyone who knew me could vouch that I was a devoted mother who only did what was best for my kids. I didn't understand why they would assume ill intentions.

It was a hard pill to swallow, realizing that my own actions could have in some way harmed my children. Being called out in a semi-public forum was even more distressing. If I had given into my visceral nature, I would have told them all where they could shove it and left those groups in spectacular fashion.

But I Didn't Do Any of That, and Here's Why...

- While I didn't want to hear some of what they were telling me, it did make a lot of sense. The term *diff-ability* did dress up the phrase disabled. It took a while to wrap my head around this concept, but by using these words I was in fact devaluing disabled people. My kids don't need some sort of superpower to validate their existence.

- I knew from day one that the little tidbits of information TopDoc fed me didn't sit right. When he handed me that script for ABA without offering one single apprehension about the intervention, my Spidey-senses started tingling. If I didn't know anything else, I knew developmentally appropriate practices. There is nothing—and I mean nothing—appropriate about a toddler sitting at a table to work, forcing them to perform tasks, and ignoring their protests (NAEYC 2020a). While I may have lost confidence in myself as a parent since Jay's diagnosis, my *bullshit-o-meter* wasn't completely broken.

- As I mentioned earlier, TopDoc never gave me sufficient explanations for my questions. All I would get was, *Oh, that's just autism.* For an expert in pediatric development, his answers didn't seem very expert. It was obvious to me that he didn't believe in my child or care about his emotional health after he gave his prognosis. I wasn't sure why at the time, but these strangers certainly seemed to. I could tell that these people wanted me to do better for my kids, and that's the type of energy I had been searching for.

Unlearning is hard. It's painful. Quite frankly it's embarrassing. So why on Earth would we subject ourselves to this process? The answer is simple: We do it for our kids. If a car was going to hit my children, I wouldn't hesitate to push them out of the way and brace for impact. If a person started shooting while we were out together, I wouldn't think twice before standing between the shooter and my children. As parents, we should think along those same lines when confronted with the uncomfortable feelings that go along with this learning process.

Autistic people have been marginalized and undervalued for decades (Silberman 2015), and our children are now a part of that community. It's our responsibility as parents to learn from that community, no matter how uncomfortable it is, to help break the cycle of misinformation and outdated stereotypes. When we model more thoughtful and respectful language in our conversations, we establish a higher standard for others to follow—including school and medical personnel, friends, and family. There's nothing we wouldn't do for our children, and I would argue that unlearning ableist ideology is comparable to protecting them from harm's way.

CHAPTER SIX

We've Heard It All Before

— JULES —

The distrust and occasional hostility that many autistic people have for allistic parents is based on historical oppression, observations of patterns of behavior, and it is reasonable. For parents who have no education or experience with autistic history, it can feel like being attacked by angry people for seemingly no reason. We hope this text will point you in the direction of more resources to educate yourself on these topics. There will be no blind trust between allistic parents and autistic people. Trust is built between individuals, not between groups of privileged and oppressed.

While this book isn't meant to be an academic journey into the history of parent advocacy and oppression of their disabled offspring, readers should understand that parents have historically been both. In the fight for disability justice, some parents have been incredible accomplices, and others have been staunch opponents against the liberation of disabled people. Most fall somewhere in between.

Accordingly, I feel both compassion for and frustration with parents of autistic children. As a parent, I understand how completely lost many feel when they want what's best for their child, but they don't know where to begin. As a disabled person myself, well-meaning parents can be the most frustrating roadblock against any kind of progress toward disabled people living better lives.

97

While there's no specific checklist that we reference to measure whether a parent is supportive of autistic liberation or subjugation, many autistic adults observe patterns of parent behavior that might lead us to feel cautious. When autistic advocates come across a parent who has demonstrated a number of behaviors that fall into the pattern of "oppressors," we may be alert to danger. This means that well-meaning parents sometimes accidentally step into very delicate conversations without a full understanding of history, context, triggers, and then they're surprised when they aren't well received.

When I first came across Meghan's blog *Not an Autism Mom* and learned that she's an allistic parent of autistic children, I felt a rush of excitement. My assumption was that her understanding of the term "autism mom" was the same as mine, which I'll discuss later in this chapter. As it turned out, she was simply resisting being put in a category and had almost no knowledge of the context her name brought with it.

I followed her blog, and I liked most things she wrote, although a few things struck me as problematic. Despite the occasional hurtful pang that I felt while reading Meghan's content, I kept reading. As a parent of newly diagnosed autistic children, I understood where she was coming from. We were on parallel parenting journeys. I could tell she loved her children and wanted what was best for them.

Every now and again, I commented when I noticed something that felt hurtful to read. I thought she, like me, would appreciate constructive criticism so that she could do better. Who doesn't want to do better? However, I rarely engaged unless I saw something that didn't sit well. One time, I reminded her that her children will be able to read what she wrote one day, and she might want to remember that when publishing things on the internet.

After a few of my critiques, Meghan called me a troll and told me to start my own blog if I didn't like what she had to say. That was infuriating. Why write publicly and share on social media if you don't want the public to read or respond? I wasn't trolling, I was helping!

This wasn't the first time someone suggested I start blogging. When I wrote essays and posted them on my personal social media accounts, people suggested I make them public so more people could read. When Jennifer Cook O'Toole told me, "Just start writing, people will read it," during a book signing after a keynote presentation, I felt warm and fuzzy inside, but I was too scared to put myself out there. But when Meghan wrote that comment, I followed through out of spite. This mommy blogger wants me to start my own blog? Fine, I'll start my own blog. I love writing, and even if no one ever reads what I write, I want to counter the harmful narrative of autism that is led by allistic people.

I created *Autistic, Typing* as an anonymous Facebook page, with no expectations.

Beware

The first thing I ever learned about autism was that autism is bad. Children with autism are unsalvageable, incurable burdens that are a waste of life. Autism terrorizes parents and breaks up families. That was the complete picture that I had of autism in the 2000s when the word first came up during an internet search when I typed *Why is my toddler flapping?* A few years after that internet search, in 2009, Autism Speaks published their *I Am Autism* video, produced to raise money for their organization so they could eradicate this horrible disease.

Be aware of autism.

Beware.

Autism awareness campaigns are not about autism. They are about the hardship that autism causes for parents and our society. They promote stigma and misinformation; they don't dispel myths that harm autistic people. Awareness campaigns made me aware of little more than how autism is a hardship and must be prevented, avoided, treated, and cured.

The autistic community is angry, and we have a right to be angry. Autistics are tired of combating billions of dollars and decades of hate speech and misinformation, just to be seen as people, and not objects or projects. We regularly experience abuse and oppression, while simultaneously being placated. We are tired. We are tired of having the same conversations with new people who have been taught the same ableist "autism awareness" trope that we are puzzles.

We're not puzzles, we're people. Allistics wouldn't be so puzzled and confused if they would work harder to communicate with us on our terms, rather than demanding we communicate their way, if they met us where we are. It is unfair to presume that people who have a disability that impacts how we communicate and socialize will be able to engage in difficult conversations as if we aren't disabled.

Autism Parents

Autism parents do not exist. It's a label that parents apply to themselves. It is a social identity that parents of autistic people have adopted to form bonds with other allistic parents of autistic children. It's worn as a badge of honor, of pride, of combat. But what exactly are they combating? What many parents don't know is that "autism moms" have historically combated the autism that they felt took their children away from them, as if we are infected by a disease that can be beaten if they just fight hard enough.

As demonstrated by Meghan's decision with her page name, not everyone who uses the term "autism parent" has bought into awareness campaigns or the tragedy narrative surrounding having autistic children. Some parents haven't had the time to go through a learning period to know what the autistic community associates the term with. This is also true for parents who use puzzle-piece gear or wear blue autism-related attire.

There are, however, other parents and organizations who have heard the protest from the autistic community and know exactly what many autistic adults think of the term. Yet they still decide to identify as autism parents because the awareness campaigns are something that they feel relate to them and their children. This is disheartening to autistic adults who are trying to fight the tragedy narrative so their children can have a better quality of life than we did. These parents and organizations contribute to the ongoing tensions in our communities.

Perhaps one of the most frustrating parts of the term "autism parents" or the more gendered variants "autism mom" and "autism dad," is that many of these parents elect to use identity-first language for themselves, while denying autistic people use of identity-first language for themselves. They'll remind autistic people, "You're a person first!" Or they'll correct us, "You're a person with autism," as though we don't have a right to choose the language we prefer for ourselves.

There was a time that I identified myself as an autistic parent of autistic children, and a self-proclaimed autism mom told me, "You're not autistic, you're an autism mom." This exchange left me annoyed, because autistic people should both be supported in our language choices for ourselves and have access to the more clear language. I choose to use identity-first language for myself, I'm an autistic person. If others choose to identify as a person with autism, that choice should be supported too. In any case, the only people who have a right to claim an identity related to autism are autistic people.

By hijacking our identities, autism parents muck up language. I am not a "mom with autism with children with autism."
I'm not an "autism mom with autism."
I am an autistic mom of autistic children.

Co-opting the identity of autistic people is confusing, and also turns a child's diagnosis into a recreational activity. Soccer mom? Sure. Dance mom? Okay. Hockey mom? Remember your coat! Autism mom? Is your child autisming for sport? What's their score? Oh, shit! That's why they use levels?!?

Linguistically, adjectives aren't interchangeable. If I have a soccer net and a round ball, the soccer net doesn't become a round soccer net because the ball is nearby, even though they are related. In addition to having a neurodiverse family, Meghan has a multiracial family. Her kids are Black and Brown. Meghan wouldn't call herself a Black mom because she isn't Black. She is a parent of Black and Brown children, just like she is a parent of autistic children.

Patterns of Behavior

When I see a parent claim to be an autism mom, autism dad, or autism parent, I am immediately weary. I suspect they've bought into the "autism awareness" campaigns. They plaster blue or multicolored puzzle pieces on their social media and car bumpers. They have absorbed the marketing message that autism is a puzzle to be solved, and there's not much space allocated in Puzzlepieceland for hearing directly from autistic people. Whereas... if non-autistic parents listened to autistic people, autism might be less puzzling.

Disclosing an autism diagnosis while interacting with parents often results in losing credibility, rather than adding to it. There's always some kind of justification for why a particular autistic person doesn't have a right to self-advocate or advocate for the community as a collective. We're disqualified from having a say, no matter who we are. We're too autistic, not autistic enough. We're too well-spoken or we don't speak. Too high functioning, too low functioning. This isn't Goldilocks, there's no "just right" autism profile that qualifies an autistic person to have a say.

So, who exactly is allowed to advocate for themselves? Judging from our experience with the prominent autism organizations, it's the well-behaved autistics who share their perspective. Looking at many parent-led organizations, only parents of "severe" autistics should have any sort of input, and only if that parent holds the attitude that they are victimized by their child's disability.

Why Are You So Mad?

Due to abuse by allistic parents, I carry low-level trauma from the backlash of parents who hate that an autistic person is leading work that they participate in. I have to sit across the table with people who would rather my existence had been prevented. I have to sit at the table with parents who see me as nothing more than a "faker" who doesn't know what it's like to be a parent of "severely disabled" children, even though they know very little about me or my children. I don't disclose details about my children publicly because my children have a right to privacy and I don't have the right to take that away from them. But my preference for their privacy doesn't discount my experiences as a parent.

Here are some examples of phrases I come across every single day while advocating in parent-led spaces, both online and in-person. No matter how often autistic people try to help parents unlearn, these statements never seem to go away. Even Meghan has said a few of these before she knew better. Hopefully you, our readers, will be able to help combat these phrases when you come across them yourselves.

"You're not like my child"

Spot-on! You're right, I am not like anyone's child, because I am an adult. I've had more than 30 years to learn, grow, and become the person I am today. Give your child the same opportunity and trust them to develop on their own schedule. Prejudice teaches us to lump people with a shared characteristic together, that they are somehow all the same. Autistic people are not all the same.

"You're too high functioning, you don't understand..."

Autistic advocacy is led by autistic people with varying support needs. There is absolute privilege in having the ability to speak. There is privilege in being able to communicate effectively. There is privilege in not having intellectual or learning disabilities. Those of us who work towards disability justice leverage our privilege to advocate alongside those who are oppressed in ways that we aren't.

And unfortunately, some autistics don't leverage their privilege. The microaggressions that target autistic people with co-occurring conditions from within the autistic community are unacceptable. We are working on this problem, but that's our job as a community to handle.

When allistic parents spend time learning directly from the autistic community, they learn that most autistic advocates are against what we label as "Aspie supremacy." Aspie supremacy is the idea that autistic people who do not have co-occurring conditions such as apraxia or learning or intellectual disabilities are somehow better than autistic people who do have co-occurring conditions. Aspie supremacy is also the idea that autistic people (those without co-occurring disabilities of course) are the next phase in evolution, or somehow superior to allistics.

Yes, there are some autistic people who think this way, and they are wrong. I vehemently disagree with this perspective, and it needs to be addressed. All autistic life has value. Our value is based on our humanity, not what we contribute to capitalism. Learn our language and support our work to dismantle this ableism known as Aspie supremacy. Don't contribute to this type of ableism by using functioning labels and making assumptions about people you've never met or gotten to know.

"but...severe autism"

Autism is autism, has always been autism, will always be autism, even when people mislabel it or want to divide our community into pieces. Divide and conquer is a pretty old trick, and we're not falling for it. What people recognize as severe autism is typically an autistic person who has co-occurring conditions, such as apraxia or movement differences.

People who are labeled with "severe autism" often endure more harm, more language deprivation, more abuse, more exclusion, more restraint, more exploitation, more violence. And because the powers-that-be continue to roll all of a person's diagnoses into a Big Bad Scary Thing Called Autism, they use it as an excuse to want a cure for autism.

Specifically, they want a cure for severe or low-functioning autism, and they want those they deem to be high functioning to just stop pretending they're disabled. And that's why divide and conquer can't work. Every autistic person, no matter their co-occurring conditions, deserves to be accommodated, deserves to be supported, deserves to be valued. Period.

"You don't know what it's like to parent a severely autistic child"

I do, actually. I just don't use that term and neither should you. I talk more about this in Chapter Eleven.

"I love my child but hate their autism"

This is not possible. You can't remove the autism from your child, it's not an accessory. Autism is an integral part of who an autistic person is. It's okay to acknowledge hard days and seek support, but not at the expense of your child feeling like they are loved conditionally.

When parents tell their children they love them, but don't love their autism, they are making their child feel bad about themselves. Teaching children that an integral part of their personhood—autism—is bad or wrong is emotionally abusive.

Just love your child, wholly and completely, with no exceptions.

"Autism is not a disability, it's a different ability"

Using euphemisms indicates you're referring to something unpleasant. All of the euphemisms that people use because they are uncomfortable with the word "disability" are not helpful. Special needs, diff-ability, etc... Nope. I'm disabled. And I need that language in order to access support, services, and disability accommodations.

"We can't have acceptance without awareness!"

This statement relies heavily on the idea that autism awareness campaigns always share accurate and helpful information, but they don't. Autism awareness campaigns often work directly against autistic acceptance because awareness is built on stigmatizing autistic traits. "Be aware of the hardship that autism causes for people who do not have autism!" They leave out raising awareness about inclusion or access.

Autism acceptance means that we will be welcomed in our communities, without having to disclose our diagnosis, without having to justify our atypicality, without our inclusion being based primarily on sympathy for our caregivers.

"You don't speak for all autistic people"

Yes, I do, we voted on it at the last Tuesday meeting.

Just kidding! And you thought autistic people don't have a sense of humor.

Actually, this statement is correct. And non-autistic people don't speak for *any* autistic people. No one speaks for all autistic people. Not all autistic people use speech, and each autistic person has the right to communicate for themselves! We all have different thoughts, feelings, ideas, likes, dislikes, and ambitions, and we all have a right to communicate those things in an accessible manner. Let's stop pushing speaking as a higher form of communication, please! Nonspeaking people have every right to communicate for themselves, on their own terms!

"You can wipe your own ass" or "You don't smear poop"

Using hateful language to insult people based on their ability or inability to participate in activities of daily living (ADLs) is about as abhorrent as it gets. No one is entitled to knowledge about another person's ADLs or support needs. Disability doesn't erase a person's right to privacy. Whether or not an autistic adult has support needs related to toileting or any other ADL is no one's business other than that person and the people who directly help meet those support needs. Don't assume and don't insult.

Further, it is reasonable that a person would not want to sit in their own fecal matter; this is especially true for someone with sensory sensitivities. The combined sensory experience of feeling, hearing, and smelling the fecal matter is miserable for people with sensory sensitivities. If an autistic person needs assistance with toileting, it is reasonable to help them clean up as soon as possible; otherwise they will likely try to do it themselves, even if they don't have the skills to do so.

How many people who "smear poop" are simply trying to clean themselves, and then try to wipe it off their own hands? If this becomes a recurring problem, then it would be best to take as many preventative measures as possible. There are adaptive onesies that zip up the back, for example, for people who may dig in their diapers overnight, and there are sensors that let caregivers know when a diaper is soiled.

No one should feel ashamed for pooping. If a child doesn't use the toilet, parents should take even more care to protect that child from this emotional abuse.

We named this section *The Worst of Each Other* for a reason. Our communities are often at odds—in policy meetings, on social media, and in our communities. This is why autistic adults are often angry. We're tired of being treated like the enemy because we happen to share a diagnosis with someone's child, and that someone is angry about the circumstances of their parenthood. We're not the enemy. We want your child to grow up in a better world than the one we grew up in. We want to prevent your child from being harmed the way we were harmed.

Parents trying to raise children in isolation will struggle. This is especially true when raising autistic children. Parents need meaningful support, but sometimes the support offered isn't the support requested. Time after time, parents tell autistic people to "take that negativity elsewhere" if the autistic person doesn't provide unconditional emotional support.

Often, autistics will provide suggestions for improving their situation, yet we still come across parents who only wanted commiseration, not to fix their problem. This doesn't make sense to me. Why choose to follow a path of hardship when there's another option? Unconditional emotional validation is enabling. It's not support.

We want parents to work with us, not against us. We want parents who question us about our functioning levels to instead question why those with co-occurring conditions aren't in fact included in more conversations. We want parents to actively make space for those autistic people. I love to see complex communicators and autistics with ID being fully included in every conversation that has to do with autism, without being exposed to ableism, hostility, or insults.

If an autistic adult has insight into being successful in a given scenario, we want parents to meet us with respect and curiosity, rather than animosity. While our community is wonderfully diverse, we share much more with your children than you may realize. We live autistically, and our experiences may ultimately help you support your children.

Key Points

- Each person enters "the world of autism" with a unique understanding of what autism is. Often, that understanding comes from information provided by people who are not autistic, and organizations that are not autistic led.

- Parents would benefit from learning from autistic adults, especially those who have the same support needs and co-occurring conditions as your child. Take classes and explore resources created by autistic people and autistic-led organizations.

- The language we use matters. Functioning labels (high, low, severe, profound, mild) and mental age are outdated and harmful. Autistic people are autistic people. Each person has unique strengths and challenges.

- The term "autism parent" focuses attention on the parental experience, instead of centering the experiences and discrimination of autistic children.

Resources to Explore

"The Inside of Autism"—online course with Kieran Rose

  https://theautisticadvocate.com/onlinelearning

The Reason I Jump by Naoki Higashido

Ido in Autismland by Ido Kedar

Autism in Children by Luke Beardon

Autism in Adults by Luke Beardon

Divergent Mind by Jenara Nerenberg

DISTRACTIONS AND PROPAGANDA

Danny Whitty

I have sharp memories of the conversations about me, the overheard worries and the concerned discussions happening right in front of me as if I were not present. The good intentions tainted by misunderstanding and desperation, the proclamations of my "diseased" condition, the earnest desire to vanquish my autism. The people I loved most in the world, who loved me the most, who surrounded me in a warm, protective, fierce aura of love and worry and hope—they misunderstood me in a fundamental way.

I have always struggled because of my autism. But I also have a gorgeous universe in my mind, so many colors and sensations and connections and delights, that I know are precious gifts of autism. My depths of feelings, my immense capacity for love and compassion, my hyperintelligent brain, my beauteous way of seeing the world—that is my autistic way. But that part was hard to see from the outside, from my body disconnected from my core mind, from my unreliable and minimal speech.

So, my wonderful family had no way to fully understand and

appreciate my autistic identity. It didn't help that vocal and conventional sources of autism "information" spread the dangerous misconception that autism is a pathology to wipe out. This harms whole families, not just autistic individuals. It deprives them of the opportunity to fully know and love their autistic family member. It is such a tragic loss.

These same voices of misinformation are also an obstruction to more widespread access to the method of communication that has saved me from a life of hopelessness. Spelling to Communicate (S2C) allows me to finally share my true self more completely with my loved ones. It revolutionized how my family and friends view me, and how they view my autism as a complex but also wonderful and inherent part of who I am. With S2C, I am now so much more able to participate in the world around me. And my loved ones can now better support and join me in my dreams. It is such a change to how my autism is treated—as a marvel, as a way of experiencing the world, and as something we can all appreciate together.

CHAPTER SEVEN

Autism for Sale

— MEGHAN —

As I discussed in Chapter Three, "parents of autistic children" is a marketing group. From the moment we type "What is autism?" in our search engine, we are being preyed upon. I recognized this right away with the t-shirt advertisements, but it took years to fully grasp the enormity of its scope. Autism is a Billions (with a capital B) dollar market (Verified Market Research 2020; Broderick and Roscigno 2021). From services to therapies, from merchandise to research, the autism market is booming! That's a fact autistic advocates are well aware of and spend an enormous amount of time and energy trying to explain to parents.

Notice that I didn't mention autistic advocates spending money on this effort. That's because they don't have any of it. The billions of dollars in the autism market don't actually go to autistic people. You may already suspect this if you've ever attempted to apply for services for your own family. It isn't easy. Most of the dollars go to the wealthy CEOs and owners of the companies that claim to help the autism community in one form or another. While the list of profiteers is way too long for this book, they include applied behavioral analysis (ABA) companies (which are almost always for-profit), biomedical treatment companies, and similar organizations that offer parents the "hope" of curing or treating their autistic children (Verified Market Research 2020).

Autism Speaks is by far the largest, most influential autism company in the world (Reiland 2021). They brought in just over

$94 million in the 2020 fiscal year (Autism Speaks 2020). Notice that I didn't call them a charity or advocacy organization like they refer to themselves on their website. I don't consider them to be either of the two. Speaking strictly as a parent and as a person who's involved within my local autism community, I don't know of one single family or organization that Autism Speaks has helped.

The wealth and influence of these autism organizations leave little room for autistic-led organizations to raise funds, making it almost impossible for them to enact systemic change that could help families and autistic people throughout their life. The money we donate during April and throughout the year would be better utilized by an autistic-led organization. They are the people who know what autistic people need. A couple of my personal favorite autistic-led organizations are Communication First and the Autistic Women and Nonbinary Network (AWN).

Messaging

When parents first learn about autism, information we consume is all over the place. When my own children were diagnosed, the doctor's office had a booklet for parents new to the diagnosis. It included the five stages of grief. Here are just a few sentences pulled from that section (Autism Speaks 2014):

> It is painful to love so much, to want something so much and not quite get it...

> Many parents must mourn the loss of some of the hopes and dreams they had for their child before they can move on. There will probably be many times when you feel extremely sad.

> Allowing yourself to feel sadness can help you grow. You have every right to feel sad and to express it in ways that are comfortable.

Ultimately, you may feel a sense of acceptance. It's helpful to distinguish between accepting that your child has been diagnosed with autism and accepting autism.

That's right. At this pivotal moment when I knew absolutely nothing about raising an autistic child, this booklet encouraged me to grieve. Cancel that. It inserted the grief narrative in my mind and normalized it. Nearly the entire text centered the parent's well-being and depicted autism as a villain, separate from my child. The only goal throughout was for our children to show as little autism as possible.

Put yourself in your child's shoes for a moment and imagine...

Growing up thinking you're disordered.

Feeling like a burden to your family.

Hearing your parents talk about grieving for you while you're in the room.

Being the topic of school assemblies each April, but not being asked to present.

Hearing the statistics about people like you and being part of an "epidemic."

Being blamed for your parents breaking up.

Being forced to swallow pills and undergo procedures.

Your mom trying to cure you of being yourself.

That's what these autism awareness campaigns are doing to our children. I know, in the beginning, it's hard to imagine our kids understanding all of that. Some of our kids aren't talking and don't seem to understand words. We've been told they may never progress. But the truth is most of them do understand, even if they don't have a way to communicate that yet (Sinclair 1993; Tucker 2017).

Rabbit Holes

The ongoing narrative that autism is an entity separate from the person distracts parents from learning how to support their children. Deficit-based assessments of autistic children only add to the confusion. As I mentioned in Chapter Five, autism is not a behavioral diagnosis. It's a neurodevelopmental diagnosis, which means it stems from within a person's nervous system. Autism isn't "a thing" that is separate from the person, like a freckle. It's all-encompassing. It's a way of being. Our children think autistically, feel autistically, live autistically.

Since the most common assessments are based on how many autistic behaviors our kids display, the only way we can measure "progress" is by our children behaving more "normal" (Prizant 2015). This rationale makes us vulnerable to companies who offer the hope of improvement or the chance of a cure and has strengthened both the appeal and the profits of a dangerous market.

The biomedical community is a network of practitioners and parents who believe that autism is a curable or treatable disease. They see autistic children as injured from environmental factors such as vaccines, or sick from internal biological factors such as parasites. This community took off in the 1990s after a series of unfortunate events which included a completely unethical and discredited study concluding that the MMR vaccine causes autism. This study was immediately challenged and later redacted (Eggerston 2010), but the damage was already done.

From seemingly harmless vitamins to industrial strength bleach enemas, biomedical companies offer parents the hope of curing our children. These companies take advantage of our desire to give our kids the best lives possible. Not only do they promise results, they create robust online communities where parents can share their successes and brainstorm solutions to any setbacks they encounter on their quest to healing. I'm in quite a few of those Facebook groups right now. Even though I don't participate, I want to remain knowledgeable of what's happening.

A parent recently posted a picture of her three-year-old son who had a one inch hive on his back. She asked the group what they thought it could be and what she should do about it. Here are all the different responses for what may have triggered the hive:

Allergic reaction (only mentioned once)

Parasites

Flagellate erythema

Mold exposure

Lyme

Bartonella

Mast cell activation syndrome

Autoimmune vasculitis

Lipo C

Low magnesium.

Here are the suggestions on how the parent should proceed:

Heal the gut

Chelating foot bath

Add binders to chelation therapy

DAO supplements

Gluten and dairy-free diet

Parasite cleanse.

Not one single time did a parent suggest an oral antihistamine or cream. Not once.

So why do I call this school of thought dangerous? Besides the obvious ongoing abuse of our vulnerable autistic children, there's another issue. It's a principle called "the amplification of small truths," and it drives the biomedical industry. It *is* true that some autistic children have gastrointestinal issues and getting those issues under control can be super helpful. It's also true that some autistic children are allergic to different food ingredients and getting those issues under control can also be super helpful. When children are in less pain they're able to focus more on their native strengths. They may stim less and communicate more, just like any other person who's in less pain (Agony Autie 2018).

If we were discussing typically developing children, we'd simply make a mental note that our kids feel better and stop buying that particular ingredient. But to parents who view autism as an illness, it may look like they're *recovering*. That's because the biomedical community does such a fantastic job pushing the narrative that these conditions are unique to autistic children. Now instead of relieving their pain, we're discussing the brain/gut connection, cleansers, and probiotics. But wait! There's more! If you combine that diet with this other product, you'll see even more progress.

These anecdotal stories are amplified to vulnerable parents who think, *Why not try it? What harm could it do? What if this one small change is the key to my kid no longer struggling?* That's a slippery slope in this community. Some of these treatments are dangerous and can cause serious damage (FDA 2019). I've seen parents talk about their child developing tics, crying constantly, and worse. When a parent reports adverse reactions in these groups, there's always something the parent is missing or doing wrong.

To an uninvested onlooker, the obvious answer would be to stop whatever they started and check in with their doctor, but not in the biomedical world. There's always a next step to try, another product to buy, or an option to combine it with some other unrelated protocol. The rabbit hole goes on forever and there's no end to the options available, especially if you have the money to spend.

The amplification of small truths gets even louder when parents stay on the biomedical path for an extended period of time. Autistic people develop on their own timelines which are often different from neurotypical people, but they do in fact develop.

I've noticed that my own children show progress in big leaps as opposed to small steps. It seems like they process everything in their head before they decide to give it a try. I've learned that this type of development is common with neurodivergent kids.

Jay spent an entire summer unsuccessfully figuring out how to pedal a bike. We tried foot guards, walking beside him pushing his knees down, nothing worked. Four months later he hopped on his bike and rode around the neighborhood with no assistance. Nick shows growth in the same way. He spent the entire first quarter of kindergarten not being able to demonstrate that he could match a single letter to its phonemic counterpart. Then one day, seemingly out of the blue, he matched all of them like he'd been doing it all along. (He probably was doing it all along, just in his own mind.)

If I had just started them on a new [insert treatment here], I would've screamed from the rooftop about how great that treatment worked, instead of giving credit where it was due. The longer parents stay on this path, the more likely they are to find "something that works," and amplify their success stories to others.

Similarly, the longer parents stay on this path, the more invested they are in the relationships they form. Biomedical companies are well aware of that. It's the reason they create communities. Parents form friendships in these groups, develop strong bonds, and cheer each other on over their children's *journey to recovery*. They call each other "heroes" for not giving up, even when their children are suffering. It's a-whole-nother world in itself.

I can't imagine how hard it would be to give all that up—the friendships, the hope, the goals, the validation. But if a parent decides to stop these "treatments," that's exactly what they risk. These communities are full of diehard believers that autism is curable and treatable. The thought of replacing a child's autism treatment with compassion and support is akin to doing the same for a child who has a curable form of cancer. It's completely unacceptable. Many of these defectors lose their entire support system.

Luckily, there's another one waiting for them. Promise.

Residual Effects

The tragedy narrative is profitable. Period. The sadder the story, the more money flows. Once I started seeing it, I couldn't unsee it. While writing this book, I watched an old episode of *Shark Tank*, a show where entrepreneurs present their businesses to billionaires (the sharks) hoping for an investment. Two mothers pitched their swimsuit business and were denied by four out of the five investors. The final "shark" asked the women to give an example of something the ladies had accomplished in business, or to tell her about a project they stuck with until the end.

Out of nowhere, one of the women said, "I have a son who just a couple years ago was diagnosed with ADHD." She started crying and the dramatic music started playing. She went on to say that her son was also diagnosed with a reading and a writing disability, they spent all this time helping him, and now he's on grade level. The final shark was moved by the story because she was in a similar situation with her own daughter. She commiserated with the participant about how hard mothers work to teach their children, and what an accomplishment it is for the moms when their kids do well. The two ladies left with an investment.

Similarly, a popular parenting blogger went viral when she posted a video of herself crying about how her child will never be normal (FCV 2017). That single video jump started her business, complete with a six-figure income and product endorsements. Staying true to this profitable formula, she released a book that further adds to the tragedy narrative. Marketed as a story of personal growth and acceptance, the title itself infantilizes her child, while the cover displays a nostalgic image of her and her son when he was a baby, before she realized autism would be a part of their lives. To no surprise, it was a best-seller.

It's like the Oppression Olympics! Whoever has the saddest

story wins all the money and attention. For the record, I know how hard parenting is. I have four children—twins, teenagers, disabled, blended family, medical issues, multiracial—I get it! Shit is rough out here. But as Ellie Hunja so eloquently writes, "We are not being oppressed by the same systems that oppress our kids" (2021). But we *are* being preyed upon by those who profit from this relentless tragedy narrative. It's important that we start recognizing and rejecting these tactics. Not only do they distract us from supporting our children in the ways our children deserve, they also impede progress for disability justice.

The Echo Chamber

Autism parenting support groups are petri dishes of contagious despair. Yes, I just said that to make sure you were paying attention. Most parents enter these spaces looking for resources and information. That's the reason I joined them in the beginning. It's natural for parents to look to their more experienced peers for advice.

In a perfect world, these groups would be filled with parents offering each other information on attaining augmentative and alternative communication (AAC) devices and financial assistance. Unfortunately, this is not the case. Instead, most of them are filled with martyrdom and self-pity, where people prefer to be validated instead of educated. The status quo is rarely challenged, and those who do offer a dissenting view are met with hostility.

Support = Agreement

Support = Being kind

Support = Safe

Support = Unconditional validation.

We join these private groups to get away from public view, thinking it's safe to share the thoughts we wouldn't want the entire world to hear. We think that these groups are only filled with other parents who understand our unique situations. And in those groups, we commiserate with each other, holding nothing back. Regrettably, the internet gives us a false sense of privacy and anonymity because it grants us neither.

The reality is that in these groups we're speaking to tens of thousands of people every time we hit "Post." Parents of autistic children include our teachers, politicians, celebrities, healthcare workers—society. An online forum with 20,000+ members isn't private, nor is it safe. Not safe for parents, nor our children. If we think about it a different way, it's more like standing on stage at a concert and telling everyone our private thoughts. I don't know of many parents who would do that. Yet every time I scroll through my phone, I see the same posts each and every day:

My child is high-functioning but he never listens.

Autism won today. How do you mommas do it?

My kid is so defiant and aggressive.

My child is 8 but has the mental age of a toddler.

I love my child, but I hate autism.

Is God punishing me by giving me a child with autism?

I spend countless hours in IEP meetings fighting for my children to be included. I attend focus groups with the Department of Education and the Alliance against Seclusion and Restraint to help protect our children from abuse. I meet with community leaders to help change their perspectives, so they can view our children as the wonderful people they are.

It's maddening to come home and see my fellow parents undermining this potential progress by demeaning their own kids online. How can we expect educators to value our kids when *we* are constantly devaluing them? How can we expect society to respect our kids if *we* are constantly disrespecting them ourselves? If we want the world to be more accepting and inclusive of autistic children, I firmly believe it starts with *us* as their parents.

But What about Parents?

Parents absolutely need and deserve a robust support system. Our mental health is important too. I don't judge parents for reaching out in parenting groups. Hell, I was one of them before I realized the impact these groups have. I know that information and resources seem scarce. For many parents, this is a brand new path and it can be hard to navigate.

I also recognize that parents need spaces to vent our frustrations and get support for the challenges we face. There isn't enough support for families in general, and certainly not enough for families of disabled children. The internet, social media in particular, provides us with an accessible avenue to engage with people when we'd otherwise be completely isolated. I've met and connected with some of my favorite people from the comfort of my own home, and I'd never suggest getting rid of that.

My argument is that large online forums aren't the appropriate setting to get that support. They're too public, too negative, and too harmful. When I'm asked about options to replace the parenting support groups, my answer is simple: Start a smaller group with a few people that you trust. Use that circle of friends to talk about the things you wouldn't feel comfortable sharing with the entire world. These are the people you can talk to about toileting, meltdowns, smearing, eloping, puberty issues, whatever the shenanigans of the day are. These people don't have to share all your views about life, but they can be there for you in the ways others might not.

Find a neurodiversity-affirming therapist/counselor if you're struggling with your mental health. It may take a bit of research, but they're out there! Many of them are neurodivergent themselves. I found a fabulous counselor in my area when I was grieving the loss of my aunt. When I told her two of my children were autistic, she automatically understood my constant state of sleep deprivation. While she was empathetic, she never once advised me to lock them in their room for the night and let them cry it out. She just kept reminding me to give myself grace when I feel tired and can't seem to get everything done. That's the type of support we all deserve.

Words like *disorder*, *severe*, and *symptoms* are pretty scary for parents to hear. Reading those dreadful, deficit-based medical reports can cause us to enter a state of panic. It's hard to envision our toddlers heading off to college without being able to use the restroom. We can't picture them living on their own if they can't talk.

The thing is, our toddlers *shouldn't* live on their own yet. That would be inadvisable. The other thing is, our toddlers don't stay toddlers forever. They will learn and develop in their own ways, and on their own schedule. Our job is to support them and protect them from harm.

When they grow up, they'll be autistic adults just like the autistic adults I learn from now. Many of them use AAC devices to communicate, just like some of our veterans with traumatic brain injuries. Others use incontinence supplies, just like millions of other adults. Lots of our kids will require support when they grow up, and that fact isn't autism specific. *I'm not sure who created the goal of "being independent," but I'm almost certain they had help.*

Meeting our children where they are doesn't mean giving up on them. It means seeing them as a whole person, broadening their access to communication, helping them figure out their unique learning styles, helping them figuring out their sensory profile, and putting accommodations in place. When we work *with* our children instead of against them, instead of trying to fix them, we end up with happier children. And *that* is a goal worth striving for.

CHAPTER EIGHT

It Doesn't Have to Be This Way

— JULES —

I t was midwinter and Johnathan was in the second grade when I got my near-daily call from the Dean of Students.

"Hello, Johnathan is here in my office. He was standing on a chair. Will you please speak to him?"

"I'll be right there," I replied, with a heavy sigh. In my mind, I thought, "Well, did you tell him to get down? Be an adult. Clearly he's not still standing on a chair if he's in your office." My office was located across the street from the boys' school. I was so frequently called to the school that I needed to be minutes away, for whatever crisis or discipline reason that the school staff couldn't seem to manage.

I changed my shoes into my winter boots, grabbed my coat, and told my supervisor I was taking my 15-minute break and I'd be back shortly. She smiled at me, with sympathy on her face. I trudged across the parking lot, across the street, up the hill to the school, and into the office. They buzzed me in without a word, knowing I knew where to go.

Johnathan was sitting on a chair in the Dean's office, swinging his legs under the seat. He smiled when he saw me. I tilted my head and half smiled at him, knowing. We both knew. There was no reason for me to be called, much less any reason for me to be in the office. I ignored the Dean.

I took off my boots. Stepped carefully onto the chair and turned to face Johnathan. He covered his mouth with both hands and his shoulders shook with giggles.

"What am I doing?" I asked him, pretending to be confused.

"You're standing on the chair!" he guffawed.

"Is this what I'm supposed to do with a chair?" I asked.

Giggles escaped between his hands as he replied, "No!"

"Okay!" I smiled, stepped down, put my boots back on, and left. I did not look at or speak to the Dean this time. I didn't have anything nice to say.

As I walked back to work, I wondered why they called me. I wondered why they picked on my son for the most petty reasons. Why couldn't they just be adults? I had other tasks to take care of during my break, and now they would have to wait. As I returned to my desk, my supervisor checked in to make sure I was okay.

"Of course!" I responded cheerfully.

At the time, I didn't know anything about disability or inclusion. I just knew that I wished the other adults could be helpful. I wished other adults knew how to communicate with my son in a way that de-escalated conflict, built relationships, and helped him learn. The power struggles instigated by adults with the attitude that children should comply "because I said so" only made things harder.

I didn't understand why people insisted on obedience without teaching or reasoning with a child. Their choice to engage in power struggles, rather than meeting him where he was at, rather than providing support, rather than developing inclusive relationship-based interventions, resulted in 169 pages of behavioral referrals in two academic years.

Caregiving

Being a parent of a disabled child comes with significant adjustments of expectations. There are also opportunity costs. From the day autistic children start interacting with people outside of the household, they experience exclusion, and it has residual effects on the entire family. Parents are often called by non-inclusive childcare providers to address their child's disability-related needs, to an extent that it becomes disruptive to a parent's ability to work outside of the home.

Too often, parents of autistic children end up in circumstances in which one parent needs to stay home to be able to provide care to their child. As my story about Johnathan's experience in second grade illustrates, this discrimination continues as children grow up and attend school. Sometimes this is manageable for families in which there are two parents, but not always. Those who are parenting alone often face much more difficult circumstances and decisions. For solo parents, unless we have strong family support, we often end up in desperate circumstances.

In the United States, the Family Medical Leave Act (FMLA) is designed to support families who need accommodations to retain their jobs. Other countries may have different laws to protect families from discrimination. But there are limitations to taking leave, and FMLA is unpaid. More importantly, the fact remains that employers who want to be rid of employees will find a reason. Ultimately, being a parent of a disabled child can result in job loss, whether it's on the record or not.

Even when disabled children are approved for community-based services such as attendant care, most states prohibit parents from being paid as their caregivers. So, when parents are called to the school or need to attend scheduled appointments, the parent's ability to work is still disrupted. This type of restriction—prohibiting parents from being paid as caregivers—is rooted in colonial-capitalism, and is a prime example of how systems aren't designed to support disabled people and their families.

Caregiving is exhausting. Our society's devaluation of disabled lives results in the devaluation of the work that caregivers provide. That's the root problem. Caregivers are often invisible, under supported, unpaid or underpaid, and overworked. If it takes a village to raise a child, it takes an intentionally inclusive village to raise a disabled child. Disabled people will always exist.

Disability is a natural part of life, and disabled people and their families have a right to inclusion. Our children should not bear the weight of our societal shortcomings.

We can and should advocate for more inclusive and supportive communities because disability will always exist. But our discussions should highlight the fact that systems are failing families, not that disabled children are making life harder for families. (I'll expand on the topic of respectful advocacy in Chapter Thirteen.) The problem is never the disabled child. The problem is the lack of inclusive and supportive communities. Communities must choose to be intentionally inclusive, and communities must intentionally choose to fund and support care work.

School Inclusion and Safety

Conceptually, special education is based on inclusion. In practice, it's often an oppressive and biased tool that perpetuates ableism and justifies exclusion and violence against disabled children. Trying to advocate for a free appropriate education for my children has been painful. There's no common definition of *appropriate*. While I view it as meeting the child's needs, many school systems view it as making the child behave appropriately, even if the child can't.

I advocated for culturally appropriate and safe services for my children. The hill I was willing to die on was demanding they get my daughter's consent before touching her. As a disabled Black and Native girl, she is at incredibly high risk of sexual violence. She needs to be taught that she owns her body, and she has a right to decide who touches her, how they touch her, and when they touch her. She is touch-reactive—this means that it is distressing for her if someone touches her unexpectedly and without her consent—and she may defend herself from unwanted touch. Unfortunately, self-defense is often reported as aggression in the school system, especially for Black and Indigenous students.

I ended up having to pull my children from the public school for their safety. I tried to file a due process complaint with the

Department of Education. Because I filed it after my children were removed from school, it was rejected by the administrative law judge. There's some kind of ruling that is exclusive to Minnesota that says that parents may not file due process complaints after their child has been removed from the school. In order to overrule the precedent, I would have to take a case to the Supreme Court. Laws like this vary from state to state, but they force parents to choose between justice and safety.

Disability isn't a character flaw, but it's often treated as though it is. Disability isn't a choice, but neurodevelopmental disabilities are often treated as though they are. How many times have you heard or said "Make better choices" to a child? What if they couldn't make a better choice? What if they were doing the best they could at the time and in those particular circumstances?

Too many school systems have invested in behaviorism, dedicating entire departments to Positive Behavioral Interventions and Supports (PBIS). These practices are detrimental to neurodivergent students, even more so for autistic students of color. Students with disabilities are restrained, secluded, and expelled at much higher rates than those without disabilities (Lives in the Balance 2021).

Autism is a neurodevelopmental diagnosis and greatly affects communication in one way or another. How much of the "behaviors" of autistic children are due to the lack of access to communication? Can you imagine the distress of wanting to communicate, but not having the tools to express your thoughts? Can you imagine being thirsty, unable to ask for water, and being punished for expressing your distress?

Mouth words (speech) are the preferred method of communication for the majority of people, but mouth words are not accessible to everyone. Accessible communication is a human right. AAC should be the very first tool offered to autistic students who are nonspeaking, intermittently nonspeaking, or have an expressive language delay. Yet for some reason, the first response to nonspeaking autistic children tends to be behavioral interventions, rather than language support.

Language deprivation is a tool of oppression, whether the language deprivation is intentional or not. Language deprivation has historically been used against people of color, particularly people Indigenous to Turtle Island and people of African descent who were enslaved in the Americas. It also impacts the disability community, routinely affecting autistic and d/Deaf people. Even students in "the best" self-contained special education classrooms experience language deprivation.

There has been research to indicate that language deprivation can lead to language deprivation syndrome, a possible neurodevelopmental disability that includes "maladaptive behavior." This research has primarily focused on d/Deaf people, yet it's reasonable to extrapolate that language deprivation can have the same effects on anyone experiencing this trauma.

Our communities need inclusive childcare and schools, with support available for children who need additional support to remain in the environment. The idea that there is a finite amount of support, like we must ration our limited resources, is akin to saying there's a finite amount of kindness or a limit to the amount of love in the world. Accessibility isn't scarce if we build it into the foundation of our communities. Support is universal if everyone is committed to inclusion.

As Meghan will discuss in the next chapter, parents and educators should take a stand against outdated behaviorist practices in schools. We should advocate for safe schools, free from restraint and seclusion. We should advocate for inclusive schools and place an emphasis on accessible communication from a young age.

Let's Talk about Behaviorism and ABA

Few online debates are more divisive than the topic of applied behavioral analysis (ABA). It seems to be the hill everyone is prepared to die on, whether for or against the intervention. Unfortunately, these debates are rarely constructive or informative. They're full of one-liners, accusations, and name calling.

New parents seeking information about ABA are often left with little more than the realization that they should do so quietly, or risk summoning a figurative cyclone of animosity.

The conversation surrounding ABA and behaviorism has far too many layers to cram into one section of a book, let alone the comment section of a social media post. Autistic advocates and allistic parents must do a better job listening to each other. Standing divided on our own hills shouting at each other does nothing to protect our children. Behaviorism is a multi-billion-dollar industry, complete with lobbyists and government funding. No matter how loud autistic people shout against it, our testimonies are no match for that type of influence.

From the moment children are diagnosed, parents in the United States are pushed by professionals, and sometimes even forced by the courts, to enroll their children in ABA. It's marketed as the gold-standard autism treatment, yet many doctors who recommend it have little knowledge of what actually happens in ABA sessions, nor have they stepped foot in an ABA center.

Behaviorism *can* be effective in shaping outward behavior, and we use it every day. For instance, we ignore people when they do things we don't like. But remember, autism is not a behavioral disability. It's a neurodevelopmental diagnosis that is determined based on observable behaviors. The presence or absence of those observable behaviors at any given time do not define whether or not a person is or isn't autistic. Autism is an integral part of our entire being.

Behavior is communication. Yet still, many professionals put an emphasis on reducing those observable behaviors without addressing the children's need for support with communication or sensory regulation. Behaviorism actually stifles communication because, for nonspeaking autistic children, the only communication that child has *is* behavior.

ABA subjects autistic children to behavioral interventions for hours each day. It's dangerous and traumatic for autistic people, teaching them that their feelings and opinions don't matter. Compliance and performance on demand are rewarded, which grooms children to suppress their natural instincts. This puts autistics at a greater risk of physical, emotional, and sexual abuse throughout their lives. Many autistic people second-guess everything they say and do, because they have been taught their entire lives that the natural way they engage with the people and world around them is wrong.

The multi-billion-dollar behaviorist industry has a financial interest in pathologizing autistic traits in order to sell their services of producing non-defective children. Their marketing strategies are so effective, the people performing harmful interventions often think they're helping the children they're working with.

Parents are the customers.

Doctors are the sales force.

Behaviorists are the factory workers.

ABA corporations are the profiteers.

Children are the collateral damage.

But who cares, because they're damaged anyway, right?

This for-profit industry operates under a colonial-capitalist worldview and economy. Enrolling one child in a 40-hour-per-week intervention contributes more than one full-time job to the economy. That one child comes with a healthy paycheck for the owners of the company. The industry is, in the main, motivated by money, not whole-person wellness. You can tell because of how often they dismiss survivors of ABA who talk about their trauma. You can also tell because of how often they shut down any conversation about risks or long-term effects of grooming behavior.

Marketing ABA as the "gold standard" of treatment, this industry weaponizes systemic racism by trying to convince parents from communities of color that equal access is the solution. This tactic motivates parents to fight for services that could potentially harm their own children. True equity means that parents from communities of color would be supported with culturally responsive practices. Autistic people of color have firmly stood against this racialized ableism. Learning from autistic people of color will lead to liberation for all autistic people. Here's what Cheyenne Thornton (2021), a Black autistic advocate, has to say about ABA:

> There are ABA professionals who push the need for ABA due to dangers faced by autistics of marginalized races and ethnicities. They argue that it's necessary for Black, Indigenous, and other minority neurodivergents (NDs) to learn to mask because it will make life better or safer when facing law enforcement or racial tensions.
>
> I can say with 100% certainty that this is complete bullshit—not to mention racist.
>
> A lifetime of subservience and discomfort is not the answer to racism, and no amount of torture disguised as therapy will make a neurodivergent child neurotypical.

As a Native parent, behaviorism doesn't align with my cultural values. Equitable care isn't about ensuring that people of color have access to the same services as white people, which were based on research of white boys, with goals developed by white parents and white researchers and white practitioners, based on colonial-capitalist values. Our children change us, we don't change our children.

Police Interactions

The summer before George Floyd was killed by police officer Derek Chauvin in Minneapolis, Kobe Heisler was killed by police officers in a nearby suburb. Kobe was a young biracial autistic man. He had a meltdown and his grandparents called 911 for help. Kobe was able to calm down before the police arrived. His grandfather told the police that the situation was under control and tried to turn them away, but the officers insisted that they go inside the home to assess the situation.

Kobe never should've needed to interact with the police. The crisis had already de-escalated, yet the police re-escalated the situation when trying to "gain control." They antagonized Kobe and threatened to take him into custody—even though he wasn't accused of a crime. This resulted in Kobe trying to elope. The police intervened physically and they shot and killed Kobe in front of his grandparents, who had asked the police not to come.

Law enforcement is repeatedly and unnecessarily called on dysregulated autistic people. Frustrated, desperate, or unskilled caregivers call the police to help them with distressed autistic people, often for lack of knowing what else to do. In some cases, caretakers aren't provided the tools they need in order to prevent or mitigate meltdowns. In some cases, calling the police is used as a threat to intimidate autistic people out of their "behaviors." Regardless of the intent behind calling the police, it too often results in the death of disabled people—and especially disabled people of color.

Calling the police for help during a mental health crisis is a manifestation of behaviorism. Safety plans, which are often developed by non-autistic people, don't list the groundwork to ensure that parents are given good information about how to support their autistic child. They don't emphasize sensory or emotional regulation. Safety plans don't often include occupational therapy, speech therapy, or accessible communication alternatives.

Safety plans list consequence after consequence, escalation after escalation. Behaviorism reigns supreme, negating the need for any other form of support. This deprives parents of access to information that would ultimately improve their family's quality of life and reduce the need for police interactions.

Law enforcement rarely protects autistic people. The inconsistency in how we are treated by police is a violation of our right to equal protection. Allistic people know how dangerous law enforcement involvement can be for autistic people. In fact, they put puzzle piece stickers on their cars, attach sensors to their disabled children, and push for cops to have "autism training." They know how quickly things can go bad.

The first goal of law enforcement is to gain control. Before they assess the situation, they are trained to control the situation. This is the part that caregivers both rely on and don't fully understand. They don't understand that law enforcement officers are trained to believe, without scientific basis, that common autistic traits are seen as "pre-attack indicators" (AUSM 2019).

For example, our response time may be different, if we are able to speak at all. Sometimes we use echolalia and repeat back what is said to us. That could be misconstrued as a confession or be viewed as mocking the officer. Our motor differences are often seen as aggressive or under the influence. Other times, we shut down and become unresponsive, which is the exact opposite of the compliance police demand.

When conversations do arise about autistic people and the police, the focus is usually on parents and caregivers calling the police on an autistic person. Conversations are rarely focused on how to ensure that law enforcement services are accessible to autistic people, or how to reduce distress and communicate with an autistic victim.

I recently attended a webinar hosted by two parent-led autism advocacy organizations, and all of the presenters were white allistic people. While the topic was autism and the police, the entire conversation revolved around parents calling the police on their autistic children. No attention was given to how to support autistic people who may need to call law enforcement for help. I raised my concern for the protection of autistic people, given the statistics that we are more likely to be victimized than commit crimes. The presenters acknowledged my concern, and in the next breath dismissed it as a future point of discussion.

This type of event demonstrates clear anti-autistic bias, and it isn't unusual. I'm sharing my experience to draw attention to the typical lack of representation in discussions surrounding autistic people, and how dangerous that can be. Nondisabled parent advocates, no matter how sincere their intentions, will never be able to fully grasp and prioritize the needs of disabled people. Non-BIPOC people will never be able to fully grasp and prioritize the needs of the BIPOC community. Autistic children of color, and particularly Black autistic children, are at a higher risk of police violence, yet Black families are often left out of the conversation altogether.

We can and must do better. When planning events, we must be mindful of representation to make sure everyone has a voice at the table, especially those who are most at risk.

I want anyone reading this to feel our people's pain. We can only reduce the deaths and irreparable harm when we understand that repeating and mandating solutions that aren't working perpetuate the cycle of harm to disabled Black populations.

All these programs that flip the responsibility for being victimized to the disabled person in crisis and present the solution as somehow being centered on wearing identification, carrying communication cards, or being known to law enforcement as a neurodivergent individual need to leave the catastrophic police encounter conversation.

We have to consider what it means to have identification tags hanging all over our loved ones letting anyone and everyone know our disabled folks are vulnerable and excellent targets. We have to approach these things better than mandating solutions without including folk who know what it means to be autistic and marginalized in multiple ways.

These people may be invaluable in crafting better solutions. I cannot emphasize enough that not listening to everyone in this conversation is costing lives. (Kerima Cevik 2019)

Key Points

- Autism is not a behavioral diagnosis. Autism is a neurodevelopmental diagnosis. Behaviorist practices focus solely on changing outward behaviors.

- We should stop trying to fix autistic children. Instead, we must focus on supporting and protecting autistic children.

- Parents should beware of biomedical "treatments" for autism. They have the potential to cause harm and death. Check with your child's doctor before changing medications, diets, and supplements.

- Our communities must advocate for accessible, inclusive communities. This includes support for caregivers, accessibility training for educators, and autistic-led training for officers.

- Conversations surrounding autism should always include autistic people. Our communities should support autistic-led organizations and advocates.

Resources to Explore

Neurodiversity workshops run by Rachel Boggan

www.thepropertiesoflight.com

Therapist Neurodiversity Collective

https://therapistndc.org

Lives in the Balance and books by Dr. Ross Greene

https://livesinthebalance.org

We're Not Broken by Eric Garcia

Beyond Behaviors by Mona Delahooke

AND WHY WOULD WE DO THIS?

Cole Sorensen

The life that I lead is a meaningful life. It's full of people I care about, activities I enjoy, work that I'm passionate about. It's also a life that requires a substantial amount of support. I'm not able to safely live on my own. I rely on help from others, including support staff, in order to get my basic needs met and keep myself from harm. None of this makes my life any less meaningful.

When parents think of their fears for their autistic child—the outcomes they do not want—they often picture a life like mine. I don't speak, I use a communication device instead. I'm obviously visibly autistic and different; I stand out in a crowd. I have meltdowns in public. I will probably need help from support workers for the rest of my life. People look at me and judge me as incapable, as inferior, as less than human. I have to fight daily to be treated with dignity and basic respect.

I suspect that one of the reasons that lives like mine, that require support, are so easily devalued is because that support is often provided in ways that strip away a person's autonomy and humanity.

I've received plenty of support like this myself and seen it provided so often to others too. This support can take a lot of forms, but at its core, it's based on the assumption that the person being supported is fundamentally incapable of handling a certain task.

At one level, this attitude leads to the supporter taking over the task themselves or getting rid of the task completely. This is how I ended up graduating high school barely able to write. My parents and teachers saw the meltdowns I had in response to being asked to write and took it as a sign that writing was something I was incapable of doing, rather than that I needed support given in a different way. I went through school having other people turn the bullet points I wrote into essays for me. I would have been able to learn to write, but people looked at my behavior and assumed that I simply couldn't do it, or that it wasn't possible to teach me. (Obviously, they were wrong, as here I am, writing an excerpt for a book. I'm writing it with support from others, support to stay on task and plan my writing, and there have been a few meltdowns along the way, but that doesn't take away from the fact that I have done it.)

But I believed them. Nobody around me seemed to think I was capable of that kind of expressive language, so I figured they must be right. When I came across someone who tried to challenge me, held higher expectations for me, it just made me frustrated. Didn't they know I wasn't able to do what they were asking? I was used to the kind of support where someone just took over a task for me completely. It had taught me to simply wait and let others do things for me. I was not so much an active participant in my own life as I was an observer.

My time working in special education classrooms as part of my degree showed me that my experiences were far from an isolated case. Students labeled with a developmental or intellectual disability were held to incredibly low standards with regard to academics. They spent a lot of the school day coloring, playing Minecraft®, or watching movies while their peers were learning math or reading. Breaks and opportunities for self-regulation and enjoyment during the school day can be wonderful, but these were not breaks. These were the core activities making up a majority of the school day for these students, simply because of the expectation that they could not handle more rigorous or challenging tasks. I remember one student in particular, who was given the task each day of putting screws into a board full of holes, one by one, and then taking them all out again. This was all that was expected of the student, this meaningless task, repeated over and over every single day.

At an even more insidious level, you see this attitude that someone is fundamentally incapable extends into how they are allowed involvement in decisions surrounding their own life. Professionals often talk about the importance of providing choice to autistic people, but then do this in only the most limited sense: "choice boards" where a person gets to pick their preferred reinforcer or reward or deciding whether to clean their room before or after lunch. These are choices, sure, but only barely. A life filled with only choices like these without the opportunity for choices like "What skills do you want to develop?" or "What do you want to do when you grow up?" is not a life led with autonomy. True autonomy isn't a multiple-choice test where you pick A, B, or C. It's an essay question where you can say as much or little as you please and there's no one "right" answer. Of course, this depends on age, but there are ways to exercise autonomy at every stage of life, and everyone is capable of and deserves autonomy.

I've spent a lifetime being denied the right to make my own decisions. It's something I now demand, because I don't ever want to be in the position of having my choices made for me ever again. It's also something that I pick up on immediately when watching the ways that family members and professionals interact with the autistic people they support. What may seem like a very minor interaction to most observers registers very differently for me, who knows all too well the cumulative impact of all the tiny ways that autonomy is taken away from someone.

Although I will probably always require a fair bit of support, I've set up my life in ways that maximize the autonomy I have over that support. I hire my own support workers, direct my own services, and make sure those supporting me know exactly how essential it is that they treat me like an adult capable of making my own decisions. I make impulsive choices sometimes, whether that's disassembling a pen and covering myself in green ink a couple days before presenting at a professional conference or taking on way too much one day and ending up having a public meltdown in the middle of a crowded IKEA. It's so easy for supporters to try to intervene, stop me from making these admittedly frequent mistakes, and protect me from the consequences, but doing so limits my autonomy and independence, my ability to learn from these experiences.

My right to self-determination includes the right to make bad choices sometimes. My supporters are welcome to help me think through my decisions as I'm making them, whether that's through gentle reminders that perhaps I would rather not present at a conference covered in green ink or suggesting alternative courses of action I could take, but if they try to limit my ability to make that choice, whether by physically stopping me or telling me no, my brain shuts down. I am not asking for anything more than the same freedoms that are given to nondisabled people. Nondisabled people are allowed to do something impulsive, accidentally make a mess, or take on too much one day and get overwhelmed. They have the right to make mistakes and live with the consequences. That same right is all I'm asking for.

I would love to see parents embrace this concept of dignity of risk and allow their children the right to take chances and make mistakes. I would love to see parents recognize that their children are capable of wonderful things, and the things that they are capable of matter much more than what society says they "should" be capable of. Every person is able to express autonomy and deserves the right to do so. Autistic lives like mine are not a tragedy, but when you take away someone's right to direct their own life on the basis of their support needs, you take away their ability to live the full, meaningful life they otherwise could. And *that* is a tragedy.

CHAPTER NINE

They're Worth It

— MEGHAN —

Reading this book, it may seem like I despise all doctors—I assure you that's not the case. I simply have an aversion to mediocrity. Doctors hold positions of power and dominance over the people in their care. They are gatekeepers of services, medications, and information. Their credentials grant them the authority to make life-or-death decisions, and their directives often go unquestioned. With that power comes great responsibility, so my expectations are uncompromising.

Soon after Nick's disastrous misdiagnosis appointment, which left us with more questions than answers, we left TopDoc's practice and started seeing the family physician my local parent friends raved about. I'll call him NewDoc. He spent nearly two hours with us during our first appointment. We went through the twins' complicated medical histories and talked about their experiences in preschool. I told him about Nick's IQ score and how confused I was that they had two totally unrelated diagnoses. NewDoc chuckled a bit while he played with them.

"Ya know Meghan, autism isn't that complicated. Nick's obviously a bright little guy."

He could tell that didn't do much to ease my mind. I guess it was written all over my face. *Complicated* wasn't exactly the word I would use. To me autism was like a labyrinth of the mystical unknowns! I just couldn't wrap my head around what it was, and what it wasn't. NewDoc handed us a referral to a psychologist who he knew would give Nick a proper assessment.

"And while we're at it, let's get Jay communicating. I'm sure he has a lot to say." <Insert more confusing looks here.> "There are some great AAC [augmentative and alternative communication] apps that can help him with that. I'll set him up with an assessment so he can try a few and see which one he likes." He scheduled Jay for an assistive technology assessment right then and there.

I almost had to pick my bottom jaw up and carry it out of his office. In one single visit, NewDoc helped us more than TopDoc did in three years. I still didn't understand how he was so calm and positive about this stuff. He never downplayed the amount of support they needed, but he also didn't seem alarmed. Looking back on this day, I realize he knew what I didn't yet—that my kids would develop in their own time. He also has an autistic son, who was just starting college at the time.

NewDoc and I talked candidly from that moment on. He was knowledgeable and genuine. We shared the belief that family physicians are well suited for families with disabled children. Not only can they see the whole family together, but they can follow children into adulthood. Continuity of care can be life-saving, especially for adolescents aging out of pediatrics. Young adulthood was a turbulent time for both me and my brother. Luckily, we'd seen the same family physician our entire lives. It was helpful to have that trust and mutual respect already established.

Nick's assessment with the new psychologist was everything NewDoc promised. As it turned out, Nick *is* autistic. She had no doubt about it. She talked with us about specific supports he might need. Since he didn't display many stereotypical traits of autism, she warned us that we could run into problems at school. His teachers might view him as a behavior problem, so we would need to advocate on his behalf. Never once did she recommend treatments or punishments, only accommodations to help him thrive.

Our society puts doctors on a pedestal. But as Dr. Barbara Stroud points out, "Doctors are only as knowledgeable as their training. Medical school trains doctors to treat injuries, diseases, and illnesses. Child development, sensory input, motor differences, accessible technology—not so much" (Stroud 2021). *Side note: Wouldn't it be wonderful if instead of Abnormal Psychology, college students took a class on Neurodiversity instead?*

Pivotal Moments

An autistic child's diagnosis appointment is one of the most pivotal moments I can think of, for both the children and the parents. I can't think of a parenting moment (past the infant stage) when I was more receptive to learning than I was during that time. I was an open book, confused about what autism is and eager to learn how best to help my child.

I intentionally use the word *pivotal* to describe this moment in time, envisioning a point guard at a basketball game. Here we are with this diagnosis and we're actively seeking out guidance to direct our next move. We're trusting our team even though we haven't seen this particular playbook yet. We're sweaty and out of breath. Wait, I took that too far...

Instead of that useless folder or the *100 Day Kit*, what I needed was an *Autistic Dream Team*. I needed Cal Montgomery to school me on my child's communication rights. I needed Lyric Holmans to give me empowerment pep talks. I needed Darla B. to help me personalize Jay's AAC device. I needed Angelina H. to point out intersectional issues that would most definitely come up. I needed the Autistic Science Person to lead me to more resources. All of these advocates are accessible to any parent, whether they're in autistic-led groups, running their own websites, or speaking at conferences. It just sucks that it took me so long to find them.

It wasn't until I found the autistic community that my understanding of autism changed. It wasn't until I found them that I returned to my roots of developmentally appropriate practices and focusing on emotional health. Their guidance and first-hand knowledge reinforced everything good I already knew about my children. Once I found them, I no longer sought out ways to fix my own children but focused my energies where they actually belong: on support, protection, and empowerment.

Parents, how much different would your perspective be right now if you had access to *The Autistic Dream Team* at this pivotal moment instead of...whatever you got?

Put yourself in your child's shoes and imagine...

Growing up feeling valued as the person you are

Hearing your parents talk about learning your favorite topic

Connecting with other neurodivergent people

Feeling proud of yourself

Learning how to advocate for yourself

Feeling valued as the person you are. (Yes, I listed it twice. It's important.)

Now that's more better.

I know some of you are reading this thinking, *But damn, Meghan. It's like nothing I say in these autistic spaces is ever right. I feel like I'm gonna get shredded if I say anything wrong. Why do they nitpick with every single thing?* That's a great question. A few years ago I asked my friend why autistic advocates insisted on correcting parents for seemingly inconsequential issues when there are much bigger fish to fry. Their explanation was unsurprisingly prolific:

Women have been marginalized and abused since the beginning of time. Rape is one of the most traumatic and humiliating experiences we face, but men don't start out as rapists. Our marginalization is systemic and we have an entire culture to combat. So, would you allow a man to walk by and grab your ass because it's not as bad as raping you?

No... No, I would not.

The same is true with all marginalized communities. The little things aren't that little when it comes to our own marginaliza-tion. But when it doesn't affect us personally, we have to learn what those "little things" are. It starts with the language we use and the language we allow, even if it seems inconsequential to us. It absolutely matters what we say and how we say it. Not only do we need to learn the appropriate language, but we also need to learn *why* we're using it and the consequences of not doing so. Unfortunately, that type of learning doesn't happen in most parent-led forums.

What's the Opposite of Internalized Ableism?

I don't want my kids growing up to think they're less than anyone else. I don't want them to hate their brains and bodies. I want them to love themselves and feel worthy of advocating for what they deserve. But that confidence starts with me and how I make them feel. I watched an interview recently with Lovette Jallow, a Black autistic advocate. A parent in the audience said her six-year-old daughter didn't want to be Black and asked Lovette how to deal with that. Lovette's answer was prolific. These are only a few of the points she made (Jallow 2020):

> You as a black mother have to make sure your entire house is filled with books of dark skin, beautiful black children... You have to make sure every single day she doesn't leave your house without you telling her how beautiful her black skin is. You have to be her barrier against all the hate because when you have a child, this is your full time job now until she actually manifests her own personality and understanding...

As a parent of Black and Brown children, every word of her answer resonated with me. But as a parent of autistic children, I felt defeated. I don't often see this type of radical acceptance and fierce protection amongst parents of disabled children. In fact, quite the opposite is true. I see parents trying to fix their kids, cure them, or worse. I see parents asking God why they were given an autistic child, wondering if they were being punished.

I see influencers "rehoming" their adopted child because the child's needs were too much to handle.

I see parents ashamed of their child's diagnosis and transferring that shame onto their kids. Some parents decide to keep their child's diagnosis secret. They don't tell their families and friends because they fear others won't accept them. They don't tell their own kid, either because they don't want the child to use it as an excuse, or because they don't want their child to feel othered or labeled.

Parent groups are filled with questions about how and when to share their children's diagnosis with them, and I see that apprehension as a reaction to the tragedy narrative we've been fed. We don't tell our children about being autistic because we see autism as bad and we think society feels the same way. When we do tell them, it comes out as a bad thing so they think they're bad. Then when the school has a *Crushing Autism* party during April (yes this actually happened, complete with a steam roller), our children feel like they deserve it because they've internalized that ableism that started with us to begin with.

Neurodiversity and support needs should always be part of the conversation, not just when we're *breaking the news* to our kids. Instead of talking about it as a deficit, we should approach the topic as a difference. All of us learn differently. My brain needs a highlighter to process words more efficiently. We all communicate differently. I use mouth words to communicate while one of my younger kids uses his tablet. We all need support in different areas. One of my kids needs help using the bathroom, while another needs help with trigonometry. Pointing out differences and support needs in everyday conversation helps normalize them.

It took me eight years to earn my bachelor's degree. After failing my first five semesters and trying out three different schools, my mom decided I needed more direct support. During the enrollment period at college number four, she spent the entire day helping me navigate the admission process. She also helped me access student support services. Not once did she remind me that I was a 20-something-year-old adult, or tell me I should be able to do this on my own. The fact was, I couldn't do it on my own. If I could, it would've been done already. I needed that support, and shaming me about that would've only made me give up.

When I finally did receive my ADHD diagnosis, it didn't make me feel "othered." I was well aware that I was unsuccessful compared to my peers who were about to graduate college. Getting a diagnosis didn't label me, it helped me identify *why* I was struggling so much. I reduced my course load each semester and took classes year round. Five years later, I graduated magna cum laude. Instead of parents hiding their children's neurotype like it's something to be ashamed of, I'd love to see us take a different, more affirming path.

The Bigger Picture

I recently attended a focus group with our local United Way, a global charitable organization that has over 1200 chapters in the United States. The representative asked us, a group of parents who had disabled children, what kind of community we wanted to see. We all said the same thing: We want to see a more inclusive and accessible community that embraces our children. When she asked us what we thought was keeping our community from achieving that inclusivity, we again all responded with the same answer: Our school system.

Before I go any further, let me say this for the record: I am a huge supporter of our public schools. I attended public school. I taught at a public school. All of my children attend public schools. As a former elementary teacher, I know how dedicated the majority of our educators are to their work. Most of them are underpaid, overworked, and have received little to no training on how to support neurodivergent students. With that disclaimer out of the way...

Our public education system has the power to change the way society views disabled people, and it has failed miserably.

Our communities will never become more inclusive if our schools continue to segregate disabled students from their peers. Children are natural ambassadors of inclusion because they all start from square one and develop on their own schedules. When some of their friends start developing differently, they ask questions and make accommodations for each other—because that's what friends do. Children don't develop an "us–them" mindset until that mindset is taught to them, whether by direct instruction or modeled behavior.

Decades of research confirm that inclusive classrooms are best for students with disabilities. Furthermore, inclusive classrooms have a neutral or positive impact for nondisabled students. With an estimated one sixth of children in the United States diagnosed with a developmental disability (CDC 2019), there should be *at least* three children receiving special education services in every classroom. If that were the case, and if those disabled students remained with their peers until graduation, I can almost guarantee our communities would be more inclusive in 20 years. Unfortunately, this type of inclusion is not happening.

Despite the crystal-clear research affirming inclusion as best practice, school systems start segregating disabled children as soon as they reach kindergarten. It's almost effortless when children are that young. Most parents don't know their rights yet, and still trust the system to act in their child's best interests. Many of their children attend special education preschool, so it seems like a natural transition. These already-worried parents find reassurance in the notion that their child will have more support in a smaller class, and the system takes advantage of that. What these parents don't yet realize is that once children are segregated, it's an uphill battle to become more integrated.

Segregated classrooms are a self-fulfilling prophecy. It's well-documented that segregated students don't receive the same quality education as mainstream children. As Jules mentioned in the previous chapter, even students in "the best" self-contained classrooms experience language deprivation. Once students are placed in a more restrictive environment away from their nondisabled peers, expectations about what they can achieve are often drastically lowered.

Most teachers are not trained to instruct and assess students with complex communication differences, nor are they trained to presume competence. (I'll talk more about presuming competence in Chapter Twelve.) These students are given far less instruction than they would be given in an inclusive setting—thus completing the problematic cycle. Each year these students fall farther behind their nondisabled peers, and the powers-that-be use those achievement gaps as an excuse to push them farther out of the system.

The inability to communicate effectively is a key factor in placing children in a more restrictive environment. Communication skills are assessed when determining a child's eligibility for special education services. It's well known that many students with communication differences benefit greatly from using high-tech AAC, otherwise known as AAC devices, yet assistive technology assessments are not standard for students with communication differences. I can't count the number of times I've asked a parent about their child's AAC device and they have no clue what that is.

Adding to the pressure to segregate disabled students, our schools are being held hostage by mandatory high-stakes testing. These tests—and the consequences that come with them—are disastrous for *all* young learners. They're disastrous for educators. They're disastrous for inclusive environments. From the moment the school year begins, educators enter a metaphorical race-against-the-clock to ensure that each student in their class can regurgitate content information taught throughout the year and demonstrate mastery of every skill. Furthermore, they're tasked with teaching test-taking strategies in order to prepare children for questions that are designed to trick them.

Standardized tests leave little room for neurodivergent learners to thrive in the classroom. In order for schools to reach minimum quotas, students with unique learning styles, communication differences, and developmental delays are often placed in remedial classes instead of being offered enrichment opportunities. Consequently, their entire school experience is often spent focusing on the skills they lack (deficit-based learning), rather than building upon their gifts and interests (strengths-based learning).

Testing companies, mainly Pearson, and other monetarily interested parties aggressively lobby our government for the continuation and expansion of high-stakes testing (Simon 2015). The amount of money our education system throws into this testing "ecosystem"—pre-tests, post-tests, benchmark tests, website subscriptions, data companies—takes away real dollars from our schools' budgets.

As parents, advocates, and educators, we need to take a stand against segregation. We must educate ourselves *and each other* about our children's rights under IDEA (the Individuals with Disabilities Education Act) and ADA (the Americans with Disabilities Act). We should use our collective power to lobby against harmful practices. We must demand that our teachers have access to the training they need to support and teach our unique learners, without punishing them for being who they are. Assistive technology assessments should be standard for any student enrolled with communication differences because accessible communication is a human right.

Real inclusion takes work. It takes intent. It takes investment. Making schools accessible to all children requires teacher training, more staff, restructuring school environments. As Jules says, parents have privilege, and we can use that privilege to make school environments more supportive for our children. Only when our schools are truly inclusive will we see that same type of inclusion in our communities.

CHAPTER TEN

High-Stakes Advocacy

— JULES —

Months went by after Meghan called me a troll. As I worked on my own projects, I continued to follow her blog. One day I left an encouraging comment on a Facebook post that she had written. She replied, saying it was nice that I gave her positive feedback, because she didn't think I liked her blog. I responded that sometimes there was some problematic content, but her page *wasn't a hill I would die on*.

It struck me that I'd been following her page, learning from and appreciating most of her content, and she thought I didn't like what she had to say. I didn't use flowery allistic language, I didn't sandwich criticism between compliments, and I didn't leave encouraging comments. In fact, I rarely engaged unless I saw something that didn't sit well.

This was another pivotal moment for me in advocacy. Someone who I thought was doing great things, and who I thought could accomplish great things, felt like I was not encouraging those great things. I realized that as much as I feel uncomfortable with compliments, Meghan appreciated and benefited from positive feedback.

Even though Meghan lacked the background knowledge and personal experience that many disability rights activists have, she had the instinct to speak out when she thought something felt wrong. She was also motivated to learn from autistic advocates and prioritize their voices. Those are the type of parents we need to fight alongside us for inclusive communities, accessible support and services, and fair policies for autistic people throughout our lifespan.

Parents of young children often feel engulfed in crisis and confusion, even more so when our children are disabled. It's hard to see past next week, let alone past our children's next birthday. This lack of foresight can lead to parents advocating for policies and supports that benefit nondisabled parents yet exclude or harm disabled adults. But the fact remains that our children will grow into adults before we know it, so we must take care to learn from the disability community about what they need.

In this chapter, I hope to shed light on a few more issues that our autistic children might encounter throughout their lives, contributing to the safety crisis we face. These certainly aren't the only issues autistic people face, nor are my discussions of them in any way complete. I will provide links and resources to further your learning at the end of this chapter.

Some of these topics may be hard to read, as they were certainly hard to write. But I ask that you sit with them and let them sink in. Our community deserves to be seen, and our hardships deserve to be recognized. When parents advocate without this knowledge, or only use the knowledge they receive from other parents, they may unintentionally cause harm to the autistic community, of which their children are a part.

The Cliff

Support for autistic children and their families relies heavily on how much parents complain and the dynamics of their privilege. Whiteness and ability contribute to financial and social capital. Financial and social capital allow access to services, support, and influence. This influence is part of a power dynamic that grants parents of disabled people more power over disability policy than disabled people. Multiply marginalized disabled people hold even less power.

Once autistic people age out of special education, there are very few services for adults. Autistic people, as a collective, are broke. We are broke-broke. We have faced the cliff of services, we have fallen off the cliff, we are often left with very little support. Occupational therapy? Good luck finding someone who will work with adults. Speech therapy? Nope, should have that figured out by now.

Not only are services limited, but we regularly experience access barriers. The entire system changes when disabled adults age out of the public school system. Whether we're applying for services or just trying to live life, there are barriers coming from people and organizations that claim to be well meaning. Applying for help? You'd better have some fantastic executive functioning skills—autistics with ADHD need not apply (for any form of government-funded support).

Many parents of older children are well aware of this cliff because their children are about to fall off of it. The cliff exists because parents typically advocate for policies that benefit parents and families and push off the needs of disabled adults because those needs aren't a barrier they are facing at the moment. Once their children become adults, all of that work they put in becomes moot. Most autistic adults you encounter online and in person have already experienced that cliff and are now fighting for support and accessibility after age 21.

In order to create a continuation of services for your children, including housing options and fair labor practices, parent advocacy should always be led by, or at the very least be in collaboration with, disabled advocates. Disabled adults know the needs of disabled adults. Nondisabled parents have influence. By working together, we can get rid of this cliff of services. We'll talk more about collaborative advocacy options in Chapter Fifteen.

Lack of Independence

Guardianship and conservatorship are often seen as the default action when a child becomes an adult. It's easier to take away an autistic person's rights via guardianship or conservatorship than it is to access any type of adult services. This, again, is a result of misguided advocacy.

As Tyler approached adulthood, it seemed to be the expectation of service providers that I would seek guardianship over him. This expectation surprised me, as I believed that people who know me are well aware of my position on guardianship. No, Tyler will not be able to live independently in early adulthood, and that's okay. For as long as he needs and chooses, he'll live at home, and he will be empowered and supported. When he's ready, I will help him transition to the next phase of his adulthood.

It's an interesting construct that the colonial-capitalist system has created. Push disabled offspring physically out of the home upon adulthood into some sort of semi-independent living situation or group home or residential treatment facility, but still maintain control over their autonomy, depriving them of agency and the right to self-determination.

Meanwhile, people from cultures around the world, both abled and disabled, live in multi-generational homes, and there is no expectation that children will move out of the family home upon the age of majority. In fact, it is the expectation that families support one another throughout the lifespan. Grandparents help babies and children; young adults help elders.

Many parent-led organizations encourage parents to plan ahead for guardianship, but disabled advocates are pushing back. There are other options parents can and should look into—medical power of attorney, educational representative, etc. It's true that guardianship is easier on parents when their children become adults. They maintain complete control over their children's medical, educational, and financial decisions. But this is not what's best for disabled adults. We have a right to autonomy, to make our own decisions—even when we make mistakes. We have a right to make mistakes.

Financial Security

Access to disability support typically requires that disabled people meet certain income limitations. There are income and asset limits, marriage penalties, and the constant threat that we are expected to be productive but we may not profit. Financial support programs like SSI (the Supplemental Security Income) claim that they want participants to try to find employment, yet they use any amount of success to cut off a person's benefits, regardless of the sustainability of the disabled person's labor.

While the benefit calculations are designed to support a person working, there's no protection for a disabled person who can't sustain permanent employment. If a person is successful for six months, they may no longer be considered disabled and lose benefits. But at seven months, if they reach burnout and lose their job, they have to go through the years-long process to reapply and appeal for benefits.

Further, laws and policies are still in place which allow Medicaid to recapture any form of wealth that a disabled person earns throughout their entire life (American Council on Aging 2021). We are allowed to earn money from work, but we are only allowed to earn a limited amount of money before losing Medicaid and disability services. Rules vary by state, but we are typically allowed to own one house and one car.

When a disabled person dies, whatever we were allowed to accumulate during our life may be recovered by the state—home, vehicle, cash, and equivalents. They call this the "Estate Recovery Program," as they can take assets from a person's estate, sell those assets, and then use the money towards reimbursing the costs that the state has paid towards a person's Medicaid costs. This potential asset seizure places disabled people and their families in an even more vulnerable position and reduces their chances of amassing generational wealth. I fear my disabled children will be left with nothing, no matter how hard I work.

In addition to being condemned to a lifetime of poverty, autistic people are often expected to volunteer in their communities or provide free labor. This type of exploitation is reframed as *inclusion*. We're often invited to speak at events that our abled peers are paid to organize, present, and attend, under the guise of *advocacy*. Again, this is exploitation.

Subminimum wage is a function of the colonial-capitalist system, and it extends far beyond day programs. We must produce something, no matter what it is that we produce. If it takes a full shift to sort one box of mail, we may only get paid $10 for the full day. After all, our disability makes us less productive, thus our time is worth less.

Worthless.

Subminimum wage and free labor are unacceptable. Disabled people deserve to earn a livable income, to work in respectful and accessible environments, and to receive the support we need. Our systems—Social Security, Medicare, Medicaid, Social Services—can change if enough people want them to change. As we advocate, we must listen to those most impacted by these policies. They know best what changes we should focus on.

Parents worry about what will happen to their children when the parents are gone. I have those worries, too. We need parents to partner with disabled advocates to fight for wages that will help their child live a full life, with safe living arrangements, liberated from poverty. We need to work now to make sure our kids are prepared for the future, so they aren't abandoned in an institution when we are no longer around to support them financially or otherwise.

Abuse

People need to understand the inherent vulnerability of being an autistic person, and the implication of mainstream interventions on our safety. Predators know of our vulnerability. So, too, should parents and other caregivers, educators, providers, and support professionals. We experience all forms of abuse at higher rates than typically developing people because of this vulnerability, often at the hands of people who are supposed to protect us.

Ninety percent of people with a developmental disability will be sexually abused in their lifetime. Forty-nine percent will be sexually abused ten or more times (OJP 1995). We don't have statistics on the risk for developmentally disabled people of color, but we can only assume that the risk is higher.

My own life has been defined by sexual assault. Due to the intersection of being an Indigenous and autistic woman, there was maybe a 5 percent chance that I would live my life without experiencing sexual assault. Sexual assault during both childhood and adulthood have altered the path that my life has taken.

More than half of Native American women experience sexual violence in their lifetime (NCAI 2018). Twenty-five percent of African American girls are sexually abused before their 18th birthday (Ujima 2018). Sexual violence also impacts other intersections of autistic identity. Trans people have up to a 66 percent risk of sexual assault (OJP–OVC 2014).

Physical abuse is often dismissed or justified based on our disability. Growing up, many of our peers push us around or tease us because we're "weird." All too often, our teachers use restrictive procedures because we're moving in unwanted ways. Many parents use corporal punishment because we don't follow directions. Some providers use restraint and electroshock when we're noncompliant. These practices need to end, and the people responsible for our care need to ensure that they are meeting our underlying needs, rather than punishing us for having unmet needs.

Behavioral interventions often remove a child's bodily autonomy, rather than empower children to develop skills related to consent and agency over their own bodies. Providers may touch children without their consent, whether it's hand-over-hand ABA, speech therapy, feeding therapy, or any number of other interventions. As a routine part of the intake process, parents sign a consent form, and children are deprived of the right to decide whether, when, where, or how others touch them. If a child is reactive to touch, the child is often forced or punished, rather than accommodated.

The end result of conditioning children to accept unwanted

touch is that they don't learn how to protect themselves from unwanted touch. Our children are being groomed to accept abuse, deprived of learning the skills to communicate consent or denial of unwanted touch. The deprivation of rights of disabled people has existed since legal systems have existed, and even the systems designed to protect us are paternalistic at best, neglectful and abusive at worst.

Ethically, children should be educated and empowered to make decisions about consent. Children need to be taught about bodily autonomy, anatomy, boundaries, and consent. These things must be taught in an accessible and culturally responsive way. This isn't happening. Instead, many of our autistic youth are being conditioned to be compliant, groomed to accept people violating our boundaries, and punished for saying "No."

Suicide

It often feels like autistic people are not allowed to love ourselves. And not even love—we aren't allowed to accept ourselves or have pride in who we are. When an autistic person says something positive about themselves, or mentions autistic pride, soon thereafter, society will arrive to remind that person about the burden they have been their entire lives. That they're probably responsible for their parents splitting up, that they're part of the population costing the world however many billion dollars to care for them.

A nearly universal experience of autistic life is bullying, and it comes from all sides. We are commonly rejected by neurotypicals within seconds of meeting, and it occurs throughout our lives. Social exclusion occurs across contexts, and throughout one's life. Autistic people are rejected and bullied by peers, teachers, parents, providers, employers, colleagues, and even random strangers in Target parking lots.

Due to the trauma and lack of meaningful support that autistic people experience, we are at an unacceptably high risk of suicide. When every day is a fight to just be seen as a human being, to be respected as an equal, the idea of not having to fight anymore can seem like a relief.

Filicide

Each year on March 1st, the disability community gathers to mourn the lives of disabled people killed by their caregivers (Disability Day of Mourning 2021). Filicide, when a parent murders their child, is the nadir (rock bottom) of parental ableism and abuse.

Every time I see a news alert about a missing autistic child, my mind automatically wonders if the public story is true, or if a parent may have caused the child's disappearance. Filicide is often presented as a mercy killing. The press creates a spectacle of how stressed the parent was, how much of a burden the child was. And due to this bias against disabled people, killer parents are offered public sympathy and lenient sentences (Perry 2017).

For some reason, the press coverage of these parent murderers doesn't include statistics about filicide or provide information about prevention or resources for other parents. ASAN's *Anti-Filicide Toolkit* (2022) should be included in every news segment or article, but I've rarely seen it shared outside of the disabled community. Filicide is often represented as a one-off problem, a mentally ill or over-burdened parent, and not as a systemic or societal failure that we must correct in order to protect our most vulnerable community members. That needs to change.

> Disability makes children more vulnerable, not more deserving of being killed.

> Murderous parents should be held fully accountable.

> Our communities need to ensure that disabled people are safe.

The topics in our past few chapters are the hills we should all die on together, so we can shape a more supportive world for the next generation of autistic people. We must start by learning about ableism and recognizing it within ourselves. This is not a quick item to check off on your to-do list. Ableism is systemic, entrenched so deeply it's often hard to see.

We must learn the history of autistic people and how they've been treated throughout the decades. We have to know where we've been, so we can break the cycles of abuse, mistreatment, and death. We must create space at the table and listen to those who are most vulnerable, due to race, poverty, culture, gender, co-occurring conditions, and more. In other words, we must be mindful of intersectionality.

This safety crisis is unacceptable. As a community, we have the means to change it.

Key Points

- The autistic community is facing a safety crisis. Our community must listen to autistic people when advocating for services and public policies.

- Our schools and communities *can* become more inclusive and accessible. Parents, working together with the disabled community, have the collective power to make those changes.

- Children who are nonspeaking or have atypical speech development should have access to a robust AAC system. Parents should ask their child's therapists and doctors for an assistive technology assessment.

- Parents and community members would benefit from learning about the history of autism and autistic people.

Resources to Explore

Communication First

https://communicationfirst.org

Wrightslaw: Special Education Law and Advocacy

www.wrightslaw.com

Alliance Against Seclusion and Restraint

https://endseclusion.org

NeuroTribes by Steve Silberman

War on Autism by Anne McGuire

The Neurodiversity Reader by Damian Milton *et al.*

"ASHA's Position Statement on FC and RPM Violates My Child's Human Rights: What Parents and Educators Should Know About FC and RPM"

https://wp.me/p8HwDT-1Cm

Cara

Michael Vonheath Becht, Jr
May 21, 1999–July 6, 2009

Remember me.
Remember me while I'm gone.
My body may be in the earth but my spirit lives on forever.
Remember me.
Remember my smiles.
Remember my mischief.
Remember my unconditional love.
Remember my hardship.
Remember my struggle.
Remember my pain and the torment I had to endure.
Remember that I still loved through it all.
Remember me.

Say my name!
Michael Vonheath Becht, Jr!
My name means something.
Remember how beautifully handsome I was.
The softest features.
The rosiest cheeks.
The longest curly lashes.
The beautiful baby blue eyes.

Remember me.
Please don't forget about me!
I mattered!
I was hard to handle sometimes. I was only 10!
I was playful!
I was so smart!
I loved apples, and cheetos puffs, and peanut butter!
I loved Raja.
I loved my sisters.
I loved my family even though they didn't
understand me or want to.

Remember me.
I was the WWE champion in my house.
I was the baseball star in my house.
I was the bologna king!

My wrestling guys and Spider-Man were all I ever played with.
I kept Raja close to me because she was my safety net.
I could ride my bike with no handlebars!

Remember me!!
Remember me!!
REMEMBER ME!

Please don't let me fade away.
I matter!
Remember me.

Mikey was 10. My sister Erica was 12. I was 16.

While dropping me off at my aunt's house in May, my "mother" Patti asked me if I wanted to go to sleep together with her and my siblings. I got out of the car and told her not to talk to me about things like that again because it made me uncomfortable. I had to stay the night at my aunt's house that night. I couldn't sleep because I was so sick to my stomach worrying. At 10pm, I walked six blocks to check on my family. They were fine.

Growing up, I was a caregiver for my younger siblings. I was the oldest, the responsible one, the nurturer, while still a child myself. They call it adultification—making children take on the role of an adult. My brother and sister were more than just my siblings, those were MY babies. I raised them. I fed them. I washed their clothes. I got my brother on the bus. I helped with homework.

Me.

Not our "mother" Patti.

Me.

In June, I was sent to California for two weeks to babysit for my aunt. They called it a vacation, but I was the au pair. I was expected to be the caregiver, the cleaner, the servant. That was my assigned role.

When I arrived home in early July, I needed a break from caregiving. I decided to spend a weekend with my cousins in a nearby town. My intuition was on high alert, and something felt off. I called our house phone and Patti's cell phone over 20 times, with no response. Worried, I called and asked my aunt to check on my family.

It was too much for Patti to care for the children she birthed, but she didn't want to give up her control over the children to their father. Patti chose to follow through on her question about going to sleep together. She murdered my brother, attempted to murder my sister, and failed to kill herself in a murder/suicide attempt. She wrote a suicide note for me to find alongside what she had hoped to be their three lifeless bodies.

Patti waited for me to leave to carry out her plans because she knew I would have stopped her if I was there. But I wasn't there. And I couldn't stop it.

You can tell me until your face turns blue that it wasn't my fault for leaving them home alone without me. But I lost a brother, parts of my sister will never be the same, and I am living with survivor's guilt.

Before his death, extended family suggested beating Mikey's ass to whoop him into shape. Because ass beating cures autism, right? I wish I had known then what I know now about autism and how dysregulated he was all the time. He had no structure, no sensory help, no one to calmly support him. I feel guilty even though logically I know that, at 16 years old, I should have never been responsible for knowing everything about autism.

But the pain doesn't go away. It lingers. It hurts so much to talk about it, but I can't bottle it in any longer. Because those I love will suffer from the bottle breaking and all my emotions pouring out at once.

2019, ten years after Mikey was murdered, with new knowledge and the support of people who love me, I learned that I'm autistic too.

I'm a mother now.

I'm a parent of an autistic child.

I'm still here, living with the loss of my brother, trying to heal from my trauma and be the mother to my children that I always wish that I had. My children will never ever have to know that pain of being unloved, unsafe, and unwanted.

Hold your babies tight.

Love them.

Keep them safe.

If you ever feel like you can't parent them safely, get help. If you think a disabled child is not being treated right by their parent or caregiver, please please help them. Mikey wasn't the only one taken by someone who should have only given him love. So many disabled kids are murdered by their parents, it's astounding. Mikey belonged in this world. He mattered. They all did.

Mikey, I remember you.

CAN WE START OVER?

Kimberly Collins

I spend a lot of time on social media, mostly on pages or in groups that have something to do with autistic people. Even when I enter spaces that have nothing to do with autistic people, the subject eventually comes up. I've come across parents of autistic children on science pages, in chronic illness groups, news outlets, and many other sites. Whenever this happens, I almost always know how parents will respond when I reply to a comment they've made about their autistic child. Their reaction isn't determined by the type of people drawn to that page, or anything that I say specifically. It always comes down to whether or not I disclose that I'm autistic before I engage with that parent.

When I enter a space and start talking to a parent, it's assumed that I'm allistic unless otherwise stated. I've taken advantage of that so many times. Almost every single time I play the role of a neurotypical parent, the other parent views me as someone that they can relate to. They see me as someone who's in their shoes and can empathize with them. How exciting it is for them, to be on their favorite site and find another parent they can talk to who actually gets it!

I still speak to these parents in the manner that I speak to anyone. I don't change my delivery, my sentence structure, or word choice. I say the same things and have the same advice that I always do. I know some of that advice can be really hard to hear for a parent. No one wants to believe that they've been doing less than stellar for their child. But even when I say those hard-to-hear things, I get met with questions instead of hostility, and the conversation continues nicely. Of course, there are exceptions—those parents who just want to be validated. Most parents, though, genuinely have their child's best interest at heart and want to hear an idea if it means their child's life could be better.

In other instances, a parent might be aware that I'm autistic. I may even start by telling them so. When that's the case, every single word that I say has a different connotation. I don't change what I say or how I say it. My delivery and my advice are exactly the same. But suddenly these parents don't see me as someone that they can relate to. It doesn't matter that I'm also raising autistic children. To them, I must not know what it is like to raise an autistic child, only how to be an autistic person.

In most of these conversations, I only get one comment in before they make a remark letting me know that they weren't interested in hearing from me in the first place, and they don't want to hear from me again. A lot of times I can tell that the parent didn't actually read past the fact that I'm autistic. Then they're no longer interested in anything that I have to say. Instead of asking questions or saying something back to me that would further the dialog, the conversation is done.

As a community of autistic adults, we need parents to learn to trust that we have their child's best interest at heart. We've been in their child's shoes and want to help the next generation not go through what we did. We need parents to recognize us as their best asset in understanding their child's point of view, but that's hard for them to see, so they dismiss us.

As we've grown into adults, we don't resemble their children anymore. But we used to. Support needs just look different when we grow up. We get called bullies, rude, hostile, abusive, and many other things. Ironic how I'm called none of those things when parents think I am allistic like they are, even though my words are the same.

The bottom line is, these parents are seeking us out for advice. There is a child that needs help, and making sure the next generation grows up with more acceptance and love is always the goal. So, if I know that parents are more willing to listen to me when they think I'm their peer instead of an autistic adult, I have a decision to make. Do I want to be seen and heard as an autistic adult, or do I want to be understood and listened to so that the child gets what we never had the chance to experience? I realize that this should not be an either/or situation. We should be able to exist as autistic adults, embrace our identity, and speak our truths. However, I don't think that announcing my neurotype is more important than helping that child.

There are times that I cannot avoid being the autistic adult due to circumstances, and I would *never* deny that I am autistic. But I'll do whatever it takes to reach that parent and get them to understand me so that I can help that child. That's the ultimate point of me engaging that parent to start with.

Even if I had to withhold the fact that I am autistic, I made the right choice for me, because that child got the support they needed.

CHAPTER ELEVEN

Building Trust

— JULES —

With humility, Meghan sent me a private message on March 21, 2019.

"Hi, I'm Meghan from *Not an Autism Mom*. I was hoping we could connect, and I could ask you a question every now and then when I don't understand something. Not all the time, but occasionally... Would that be alright?"

I was both a little suspicious and excited. Due to the mistreatment I've experienced by allistic parents, I was hesitant. The vulnerability of reaching out to a stranger who hadn't been overly nice to her because she wanted to learn took courage and humility. Both are traits that I really appreciate in other people. I loved that she was an allistic parent, actually following through with the common advice to reach out to autistic people with questions.

Meghan continued to ask me questions about information she came across and content she shared. She too looks at issues through an intersectional lens since her family is racially diverse. Over time, we developed a mutual respect for each other and began collaborating on projects.

Accomplices, Oppressors, and Everyone in Between

I've had the pleasure of working alongside some incredible parent advocates, both autistic and allistic. The majority of my friends are parents of autistic children, and we have fulfilling relationships of mutual support and appreciation. Jean and Maren are my closest allistic friends and I lovingly refer to them as *Fairy Boardmothers*. Both are parents of autistic people. We are real-life friends who group chat, spend time together, our children play together (or next to each other), and they help me interpret confusing allistic social interactions.

Jean is a leader whose reputation precedes her at the Capitol and beyond. She's one of the most compassionate and humble disability advocates that I've had the pleasure to learn from and work alongside. She runs interference in spaces that are hostile to disabled people, preparing and making space for disabled people to lead.

Her disabled son is an adult with complex developmental disabilities, and she's been working through systems and advocating for a more inclusive community for his entire life. She hates systems as much as I do but seems to know how to work through them effectively and generously shares her expertise whenever she can.

Maren is the executive to my function, the lawful good to my chaotic good, the policy to my advocacy. She's a kind friend who always has a compassionate ear and a friendly suggestion when asked. We work closely together on many different groups and projects. As we've gotten to know each other, she's learned to anticipate when I might be a good fit for something, and when I may need support with something. She offers me information, opportunities, and suggestions—accompanied by her projections of the benefits and risks of possible outcomes. She's protective of me, but more than that—she supports me making informed decisions for myself.

When I work with allistic people, I often feel guilt and shame for the things that I struggle with—particularly things that require executive functioning. Working with both Maren and Jean over the past several years, I have always felt respected, empowered, and valued. I also support them. Whether it's helping them understand their autistic kid, warning them of a potential landmine, providing an idea or insight, our friendships aren't one-sided. Our friendships also aren't based on what we do to help one another, we are friends because we genuinely like each other. I am deeply grateful for their friendship and their work.

I have also had the displeasure of working against parents who hated me for no reason other than my diagnosis. Or maybe my hair. These parents believe autistic people should be prevented, cured, or removed from society. They push for institutionalization, restraint, and seclusion. They believe that only certain people should have help, based on a false model of scarcity, believing themselves to be the arbiters of what a valid disability is. They abuse disabled people, whether they are bullying an autistic advocate in a boardroom or emotionally abusing an autistic person for being "low functioning."

> They don't want to do the hardest work in advocacy: to build their child up, against the ableist, normalizing, conforming society. (Amy Sequenzia 2017)

As I mentioned in Chapter Six, most parents display characteristics of both accomplice and oppressor. These parents aren't malicious. They genuinely love their children, although they may be misguided or uninformed. They've spent their parenthood listening to those they've been led to believe are experts. Most of these parents have never had a reason to question what they've learned about disability, until they had to start advocating for their child.

This frequently leads to defensiveness and contempt when someone swoops in to say, "You may want to reconsider," particularly when that someone is someone else who's like their child—but definitely not like their child. It can be hard to learn that our good intentions aren't what is actually best for our children. I can't count how many times I've heard parents say that they've "never thought of it that way," in regard to understanding that ableism—not disability—is the real problem that needs to be fixed.

Parents are so conditioned to fight that we feel like we're prepared to take on the world to do what we feel is best for our kids.

These parents are so used to fighting that it often turns into a fight for power *over* the child, rather than a fight for power *for* the child.

Fighting for understanding

Fighting for accurate identification of disabilities and needs

Fighting for accommodations or modifications

Fighting for services

Fighting insurance

Fighting for disability funding

Fighting for a free appropriate public education

Fighting for inclusion

Fighting against disciplinary actions that are rooted in punishment rather than teaching

Fighting for approval of disability equipment.

I know what it's like to sit through four full days of unbearable evaluations, answering hundreds (thousands?) of questions about my child and how they experience and interact with the world. I know what it's like to listen to the neuropsychologist utter the words "severe" and "won't be able to…"

I know what it's like to complete hours-long evaluations, detailing my child's support needs for their activities of daily living (ADLs). The balancing act of saying enough so my child will qualify for services, but not so much that my child feels violated by my disclosures.

I know what it's like to fight for a "free appropriate public education" (FAPE). I know what it's like to hear teachers tell me that my child doesn't belong in mainstream school, and the special education department believes they should be segregated. I know what it's like to feel venom coursing through my veins when my child experiences restraint and seclusion in school.

I know what it's like to be scared of my child eloping, or being hit by a car, or drowning. I know what it's like to fear police interactions with my disabled Black children who have a hard time responding to questions they don't understand and can't follow multi-step directions.

I know what it's like to fight for services. I know what it's like to not know what I'm supposed to do to help my child. I know what it's like to need a personal care assistant (PCA), and not have a PCA or have an unreliable PCA. I know what it's like to not sleep because my child can't sleep and I'm the only one there.

I know what it's like to lose income because caring for my child is more important than being at work. I know what it's like to worry about the future and what will happen to my child when I'm not here.

I know what it's like to just want a break from fighting... for once.

I know what it's like to not get a break.

I know. I know that pain intimately.

I know what it's like to experience these things as a parent, *while also being autistic*.

I know what it's like to have hurt feelings because of the humiliating way people talk about people like me. I know what it's like for people to evaluate my level of functioning without even knowing me.

I know what it's like having to deal with the access barriers of having to ask for clarification about what the questions are actually asking, because even autism evaluations don't use clear and concise language.

I know what it's like to have to make phone calls and navigate bureaucracies that make me cry and shake because, won't someone *please* just help me with this?

I know. I'm right here with you. And I'm reaching out to ask you to join me in choosing a life in which we acknowledge the hardships of an unaccepting and unaccommodating society, and work towards making it less difficult for all of us, throughout our entire lifespan. Because I also know that autistic people can lead fulfilling and good lives, as long as we are provided the support we need and choose.

For parents of autistic children, it can be tough to enter a space where you feel like you might be attacked for saying the wrong thing, especially when you feel that you have good intentions. That's completely understandable. Sometimes, the things that you hear may sting, particularly when you're a loving parent who wants what is best for your child, and you're just following what a professional with academic credentials told you.

It sucks to hear that you may be unintentionally causing harm, but sometimes, you're going to unintentionally cause harm. All parents do, there's no getting around that. But when we know better, we can do better. Autistic adults are here to share their experiences, their perspectives, and their advice.

> *Show your appreciation to the autistic people who educate you.* Even if you're learning something that's difficult to learn, thank them for sharing their vulnerability and time to try to make life better for your child.

> *Do not demand that autistics communicate with you a certain kind of way, with a certain kind of tone.* Remember that autism and communication differences go hand in hand. It is hard enough for many of us to communicate at all, without worrying about how we're coming across. When we spend time educating parents, we are often opening ourselves up to painful memories and past traumas. It can be emotionally dysregulating when we're trying to protect kids from harms that we ourselves have experienced.

> *Assume every autistic person you come across is dealing with a substantial amount of trauma.* Being autistic in a world designed for allistics can be traumatic in and of itself, even without any specific traumatic events. Most of us are so deeply traumatized by the ableism that we've experienced our entire lives, oftentimes not even knowing that we were experiencing ableism, that we would do anything to

protect the next generation of autistic people from the pain that we have experienced.

Become friends with autistic people. Not in a weird tokenizing "I should have autistic friends" way...but when you happen to come across autistic people that you think would be cool people to know, reach out. Having autistic friends will help you become a better parent to your autistic child. Having autistic friends will help your child feel reassured that autism isn't something that is "other," it is just part of life. It is good and healthy for autistic kids to know autistic adults.

Find parent role models who have autistic engagement and support. Not an Autism Mom and Diary of a Mom are both fantastic allistic parent role models with public blogs. Most of the contributors of this book are also parents. As we discussed in "Before You Start Reading...," this book is a starting point. Keep learning. Check out the References section of this book. Follow autistic people on social media. Go to your local Disability Day of Mourning event (even better—donate and volunteer). Check out and support events and organizations that are led by autistic people. Learning is a lifetime adventure.

Autistic Parents of Autistic Children

When I became a parent, I fell into the traps of how to parent correctly. I tried to find the right way of parenting and tried to follow the rules exactly. This is not a healthy way to parent! I tortured myself trying to do everything correctly. I ended up becoming so overwhelmed in my attempts to meet all of the demands of everyday life that I was not the parent my children needed.

Everything I was doing as a parent was inconsistent with my culture because Ojibwe people know that there's not one right way to live. Ojibwe life is meant to be lived in a good way, based on our teachings, which are relative to time, place, circumstance. Because with the relational worldview, everything is related.

Before becoming a parent, I imagined we'd have family dinners at the table every night. I planned on having a bedtime routine that included brushing teeth and reading a book together before my child sweetly drifted off to sleep. Our home would be a place of respite, relaxation, and rejuvenation.

Once I became a parent, I quickly realized that some children don't sit down to eat. They take a bite in passing, and as their parent, I do my best to make sure that they get enough nutrition and don't eat too much junk. There are some kids who don't like being read to, and I learned that it's hard for me to read aloud for very long. And as it turns out, brushing the teeth of a toddler is more like octopus wrangling, and should absolutely qualify as an Olympic sport.

I'm pretty sure no child of mine has ever drifted sweetly off to sleep. They crash quickly and unexpectedly, and sometimes in strange places. A few years ago, I was terrified that my youngest had eloped and was missing. In a panic, I checked with the neighbors and we all started looking for her. *Where was she?* Fast asleep on the floor behind the couch that she had pushed out just enough to make space for her tiny self. She was such a heavy sleeper that she'd slept through my yelling her name throughout the house.

If you're a parent, you know the judgment that comes from people who are not parents. This has nothing to do with autism, and everything to do with people not having a complete understanding of day-to-day life as a parent. Nobody is a better parent than a person who doesn't have any kids.

In autistic spaces, autistic adults who aren't parents may not understand the experience of parenting an autistic child. Yes, all autistic adults were autistic children at some point, and parents need to learn from autistic people—both parents and not-parents—about the autistic experience. Autistic parents of autistic children have multiple perspectives, which is a great reason for allistic parents to include us in discussions and learn from our experience.

Autistic parents are often removed from parent-led spaces without mention—meaning they're removed quietly, without the other participants knowing they have been removed. This leaves remaining members with the limited perspective and advice of non-autistic parents. I should have kept score of all of the parent groups I've been kicked out of, because it's been a lot. There's a predictable pattern that occurs. As we've talked about throughout the book, the only narrative allowed in many parent groups is "unconditional support." If you counter that narrative, you aren't welcome.

The elimination of autistic parents from "autism parenting" groups is not only detrimental to the learning of non-autistic members. It's also detrimental to autistic parents. Access to services relies so heavily on social capital (who you know and what they know) that parent groups are often the first place to learn what services exist and how to access them. By removing the autistic parents, they made the very discriminatory decision that autistic parents should not have access to information, resources, or support, because we made the allistic parents uncomfortable, even without breaking rules.

And thus was born *MN Autistics and Allies*, a small group meant to center the lived experiences of autistic people, a place where autistic people could engage authentically and find local support and resources. In the beginning, it was an intimate group of autistics and parents of autistic people, and over the years it's grown to include advocates, educators, and professionals.

As non-autistic parents, it's important to support and boost the messages of autistic parents—whether online, locally, in policy meetings, and everywhere else. Be mindful of how autistic parents are being treated in the spaces you join, and the meetings you attend. Speak up for autistic parents and let others know that you value our perspectives.

Respect Goes Both Ways

We can hear you when you're talking about your child, because many of us are parents, too. The things you're saying about your kid are the same things you're saying about our kids, and about us. Choose to use language that is humanizing, whether you're online, or advocating in your state capitol. We can have difficult conversations about hard things in a way that is respectful of the people we care about. Here are some examples of respectful language choices:

Disorder/Disease ⇨ Disability/Neurotype

Symptoms ⇨ Traits

Learning deficits ⇨ Learning differences

Not potty trained ⇨ Incontinent

Severe autism ⇨ High support needs

Profound autism ⇨ Co-occurring conditions

Autism sucks ⇨ My expectations weren't met

Disability (negative) ⇨ Disability (neutral)

These words don't change reality. But they absolutely change our perceptions, how we react to situations, and how we approach our children. Using respectful language to talk about our children sets a higher standard for those around you to do the same.

#AutismMoon

Today, your child was diagnosed with autism.

Maybe it came out of the blue.

Maybe you already knew.

Maybe you fought for a diagnosis.

But today was the day it became official. It may have come with a "level," or maybe the doctor didn't feel it was necessary to share that with you today, so you'll wait a month for the official report. But today, the news is sinking in and you are shaken. Autism has entered your life, and it's here to stay.

What does this mean for your child? For you? For your family? For your finances? What do you need to do? How do you help support your child? Who can guide you? Why isn't there a flowchart (or is that just me)?

Your mind is racing and you just need someone—anyone—to tell you what to do. The only response to alleviate the anxiety is action.

I have been here three times. I've experienced the gamut of emotions.

Here's what to do:

Breathe.

Enjoy your child exactly as they are. Your child is still exactly the same adorable, brilliant, lovable child that they were before diagnosis. Never lose sight of that.

As a parent, you've always done everything you can to protect your child, and that doesn't end with an autism diagnosis. Protect your child's privacy and bodily autonomy. Learn how to speak about support needs in a way that will not be hurtful to your child, should they overhear you.

Get comfortable with being uncomfortable.

Learn about autism from a variety of perspectives, including professional, parent, and especially #ActuallyAutistic perspectives.

Read blogs, watch vlogs, sign up for Google alerts, borrow every book about autism in the library (I did), join Facebook groups (there are some fantastic groups out there that are led by autistic people).

Ask questions. Make sure you ask autistic people, not just doctors or other parents.

If you want to understand your child, learn about how they

experience and perceive the world. Learn about how your child learns (bottom up vs. top down).

Before committing to any therapy or treatment, read about the history and perspectives of the practitioner and autistic people.

Soak in all of the information you can find. Examine what seems accurate or inaccurate for your child. Mull it over, sit with it, place yourself in your child's shoes. Maybe even get an autism evaluation yourself if you find yourself in what you're learning (it is incredibly common for adults to learn that they are autistic after their child is identified).

Dedicate the first year after diagnosis to learning, without committing to anything other than improving your child's safety and quality of life. This is your learning time. You've heard of honeymoons and babymoons? I propose an #AutismMoon.

Think about swimming lessons and water safety because autistic children have a higher risk of drowning.

Consider how you'll support your child's self-preservation skills—including their bodily autonomy, and teaching boundaries and consent—because autistic children have a higher risk of abuse.

You can't support an autistic person if you don't know anything about autism. Well, you can, but you'll flub it up, and it'll stress everyone out. So go easy on yourself and go easy on your child. Autism is not an emergency!

Autism is a neurodevelopmental disability. A neurological classification if you will. It's not a disease or an illness. There is no expiration date on the diagnosis. Your child is not going to be more or less autistic based on whether or not they started a specific therapy at a certain age. Don't allow a profitable industry to push you into an action that you have not researched thoroughly. If the autistic community says something is harmful, listen and research. If the autistic community says something is helpful, listen and research.

Your child is going to be okay, and it will be because of your love and willingness to advocate for their best interests.

So, take another big breath. You are not alone. Your child is not alone. There's a community waiting to welcome you both.

CHAPTER TWELVE

In the Passenger Seat

— MEGHAN —

I've had quite a few epiphanies since I started learning about autism, all of which led me to create this book with Jules. When I took my kids on their first public library outing, I decided to check out the autism section. Most of the books had words like *overcoming* or *healing* in the title, which I wasn't interested in, but I did spot *NeuroTribes* written by Steve Silberman (2015) sitting on one of the shelves. It's a book I've wanted to read for a long time, but I kept putting it off because it was intimidatingly thick.

I wanted to educate myself on how we arrived at this point in relation to services, knowledge, and straight-up confusion in the autism world. Like why aren't AAC devices more normalized when the technology has helped so many people? I didn't even know what they were until Jay was four. Also, why didn't TopDoc mention autistic adults when so many of them are advocating in our community? I had a thousand questions and *NeuroTribes* was the one book almost everyone recommended to gain a better understanding.

Luckily, in 2018 the stars were aligned with an upcoming lazy summer and plenty of down time, so I decided to take it on as a project. I knew I'd need some help getting through it, so I started a Facebook group and asked if anyone would be interested in reading it with me. I figured maybe a dozen people would join, which would be plenty to help keep me on track. Two weeks later when we started the first chapter, my spur-of-the-moment summer project had over six hundred members and *That Au-Some Book Club* was born.

Our group took three months to read *NeuroTribes* and our conversations went all-in. It was incredible to meet so many active learners from all walks of life. Autistic advocates guided us throughout the discussions, sharing their insights, while teachers, doctors, and parents like myself learned about the horrific treatment of autistic people throughout history.

Reading this book reminded me of the first time I visited the Holocaust Memorial Museum in Washington DC. The images were so sickening, I began to vomit halfway through the tour and had to be escorted to the clinic. Similarly, each chapter of *NeuroTribes* induced such strong emotions, not all of us were able to push through.

About halfway through the book, I felt this intense mind shift. If I were in a cartoon, an enormous lightbulb would've popped up over my character. We were reading the chapter titled "Fighting the Monster." Silberman details the major players in the autism field, and how they steered the narrative throughout the past decades. I don't want to spoil the plot, but some of those privileged white men pretty much faked their credentials and inserted themselves wherever they could as fancy experts. They framed the entire conversation around autism for their own financial gain. *I'm detecting a pattern here.*

I was like, Whoa. Mind. Blown.

It was like stepping into another dimension with this new information. The world seemed so much bigger, and I realized just how little I actually knew about autism and disability justice. Yet here I was in all my privilege doing the exact same thing those men did. While I wasn't acting like I had all the answers or gaining anything financially, I was in fact sharing, advocating, and even leading without fully understanding the consequences of my actions. I vowed at that very moment to do better and use my privilege more responsibly. It's been two years since I read *NeuroTribes* and I've spent that time listening, learning, and boosting as many autistic voices as possible.

#AmLearning

Mikhaela Ackerman was the very first live guest we hosted in That Au-Some Book Club. She and her mother wrote a book together called *The Edge of the Playground* (Ackerman Willis and Ackerman 2019). Mikhaela's blog was actually one of the first sites I stumbled upon when I found the autistic community. She wrote an article about how she experienced grief as an autistic person (Ackerman 2018). While grief wasn't a subject I was interested in at the time, I picked up other insights I could relate to my kids. She talked about **fisting**, a term I'd never heard before, but something Nick did all the time when he was stressed. That may seem like an insignificant piece of information, but not to a mother of twins recovering from trauma.

The idea of **emotion regulation** was foreign to me. Until this point, every therapy or appointment was directed at my kids' outward behaviors or trying to "catch them up" to their peers developmentally. There was no mention of co-regulation or reducing stressors. It wasn't until I read a book recommended by autistic people—*Uniquely Human* by Dr. Barry Prizant (2015)—that I understood the importance of emotional regulation in my children. I learned that autistic kids experience more discomfort, confusion, and anxiety than non-autistic kids. It's hard for them to regulate their emotions in a world that doesn't often attempt to accommodate them.

The same is true of **sensory regulation**. Learning about overstimulation, understimulation, proprioception, and interoception were essential to supporting my children. Thankfully I had a much better understanding of sensory differences after reading *Beyond Behaviors* by Dr. Mona Delahooke (2019), another autistically recommended book. My children's sensory differences were never even addressed, outside of seeing the occupational therapist who TopDoc was hellbent on discrediting.

I learned about **presuming competence** and the risks to my own children for not doing so (Sankar *et al.* 2021; Tziavaras 2021). Presuming competence means to assume a person has the capacity to listen, understand, and comprehend, even if they don't show evidence to support that assumption. Even after reading *The Reason I Jump* (2013), and believing my children were way more competent than their test scores indicated, I still didn't understand what presuming competence looked like in practice.

As a teacher, I was trained to use data to drive my instruction. Once a student mastered one skill, I would move on to another skill. This basic teaching model can be disastrous for neurodivergent learners. Many of them have spiky profiles, movement differences, and dysregulation that prevent them from "showing what they know." This is why so many disabled students are pushed out of mainstream classrooms, and only work on basic reading, writing, math, and life skills until they age out of the system (Allnutt *et al.* 2019). Ido Kedar writes about his experiences of being presumed incompetent in his book *Ido in Autismland* (2012).

Gone Fishing

"Give a man some fish and he'll eat for a day. Teach a man to fish and he'll never go hungry." Learning the term **own voices** has been life-changing for me, as well as my family. Until relatively recently, most books about autism were written by non-autistic people who offered their own narratives on autism. It's a long-standing theme—non-autistic people claiming to know all about autistic people without any input from autistic people themselves.

As much as I appreciate the one-to-one mentorship that many autistic advocates have given me, I also realize their time is valuable and it isn't an efficient way of teaching. Own voices books are written by authors of marginalized communities from their own perspectives and, as it turns out, there are hundreds of titles I can choose from and start "fishing" myself. What's more important is I can learn at my own pace, digest the information in my own time, and I can come back to these resources if I ever need to look something up again.

Own voices aren't just limited to books. One of my all-time

favorite resources to share with teachers and family members is a comic strip called *Understanding the Spectrum* by Rebecca Burgess (2019). All across the web and on every social media platform, autistic adults are sharing their stories. Each contributor of this book either has a website, social media account, or is somehow involved in advocacy.

Reading Kieran Rose's article "An Autistic Burnout" (2018) caused another lightbulb to light up above my character. Toddlerhood regression is one of the key indicators that professionals look for when diagnosing autism, which always confused me. My children never experienced regression because they were delayed from the start.

In his article, Kieran argues that autistic burnout (what professionals and parents refer to as regression) is in fact related to stress and trauma. When autistic people become too overloaded, these regressions are a way for the autistic brain to protect itself. In other words, it goes into survival mode. It finally made sense! My children spent the first few months of their lives in the NICU (the newborn intensive care unit), suffering the nonstop trauma that comes with the NICU experience. It's not that my kids didn't regress, it's that they were dealing with autistic burnout since they were babies.

Kimberly Collins helped me further understand this response by comparing autistic burnout to hypothermia. When we become too cold, our bodies restrict blood flow to our extremities in order to protect our more important organs. In autistic burnout, the brain cuts off what it deems as unnecessary functions—speaking, processing language, activities of daily living, executive functioning, or anything else.

No doctor has ever mentioned the phrase "autistic burnout" to me, as it doesn't follow the medical model of disability. As a parent, I understand the urge to push through these periods. It's almost a knee-jerk reaction, as we expect our kids to follow a continuously forward trajectory. Professionals and teachers add to this pressure, using words like "attention-seeking" and "defiant" to describe their behavior. No matter what they call it, we as parents should react to its outward signs in the same manner—with compassionate, patient, and trauma-informed approaches.

Our number one job is to protect our children from harm, even when these harmful practices are suggested by the professionals we were taught to trust. Nobody likes to move backwards, especially our kids. Hearing negativity, being pushed beyond their limits, feeling the frustration in our voices—all of that adds extra stress and compounds the trauma they're already dealing with. So, when our kids experience periods of burnout, we should choose how we react with the utmost care.

Lesson Learned

Have you ever seen the movie *Groundhog Day*? It's classic. This weather forecaster wakes up each morning in the same bed, with the same song playing on his alarm clock. At first he thinks he's experiencing déjà vu, but he eventually realizes he's stuck on a continuous loop of reliving February 2nd over and over again. No matter what he does or how hard he fights, he wakes up day after day in the same bed, with the same song playing on his alarm clock. That movie pops in my mind whenever I see new parents entering autistic spaces desperate for answers, touting nothing but misinformation.

I was one of those parents when I first started my blog. While I thought of myself as a nonspecific parenting blogger, I metaphorically entered autistic space the moment I started writing about autism. I use the term *autistic space* with the military in mind. Jets who enter our country's airspace without permission can be shot down because they're considered threats. My very public words and opinions had an impact on the autistic community, whether I knew that impact or not.

I chose to talk before I listened. I chose to speak over a marginalized group instead of uplifting their own voices. At the time Jules found me, I was following in the footsteps of other moms who wrote books about curing their children using bleach enemas, and of those who described their kids using words like aliens or robots. I just didn't know it yet.

The phrase "Nothing about us without us" (Charlton 2000) was created for a reason. The moment "autism" moves past our lips, we should choose our next words very carefully. This principle applies to parents in advocacy organizations, educators in the public school system, and anchors on news outlets. Every word we choose has an immediate impact on the autistic community as a whole, and that includes our children (Bilokonsky 2021).

In the early years, it's hard to imagine our kids all grown up and being part of a community we know very little about. When Jules first warned me that my children might one day read my posts, I couldn't see past the following day. But it's true—our children will grow up and are the tiniest members of the autistic community.

Day after day autistic adults are educating and advocating for the rights that many of us take for granted. They're doing this work so that the next generation of autistic children, our children, can grow up with less trauma and abuse than they endured. Most of the time they're doing this work for free, and the work they're doing won't even benefit themselves. If we're not learning from them and boosting their message, we shouldn't speak on the topic at all.

As our group finished reading *NeuroTribes*, we had grown to nearly a thousand members. Thankfully Mikhaela eased me into the interview process because we decided to ask more authors to come speak. To our complete surprise, almost every single person we've invited has been happy to join us. In only two short years, That Au-Some Book Club has grown to over eight thousand members and we've hosted over 30 guests—from authors to activists and everyone in between. All of our guests are invested in educating parents and helping them become more compassionate and understanding of their children, which is the kind of support I wish I had had in those early months after diagnosis.

When we're not chatting it up with celebrity guests, our group is hard at work developing resources for parents, educators, doctors, and other professionals. We're constantly updating our "100-ish" book list (Not an Autism Mom 2020) and our children's book list. We recently developed a printable, one-page book list for professionals to place in their resource centers, waiting rooms, and informational packets (Not an Autism Mom 2021)—*hopefully placed in front of that dreadful 100 Day Kit... Just a thought.*

Becoming an Ally

How can parents become better allies for the autistic community? I'm asked this question a lot, and my response is always the same: Ask that question in an autistic-led forum. It's up to the community to determine their needs and goals. Only they can determine what's helpful or harmful. My *real* answer is way more complicated than the inquiring person probably bargained for, so I usually keep it to myself. I do, however, have my own reflections on allyship that I want to share, *and since it's my chapter...*

Honestly, it bothers me when people and organizations who don't belong to the marginalized group in question claim the title of *ally*. I see people on a daily basis identifying that way when I know damn well that their rhetoric isn't in line with the community's goals. These people join political organizations and lobby for services that autistic people would never want. They publish books that infantilize autistic people, portraying them as a burden. Seriously, that shit makes me cringe.

Most people think of the word *ally* in its noun form, like it's a badge or an accomplishment. *I want to be a great ally! I'm a fierce ally!* The actual members of those marginalized groups don't need any more nouns. They need verbs. They need active participants who bring all their privilege to the table and shove it around like Big Momma in the buffet line. They need accomplices who aren't afraid to risk their positions, their platforms, their status, their sponsorships—to boost the message that the community decides the world needs to hear.

Here are a few simple scripts that non-autistics can use in everyday life when conversations about autistic people arise:

- *I'd like to hear from an autistic person on this.*

- *Has anyone researched what the autistic community's opinion is?*

- *I read this article written by an autistic person who is also a professional in this field. This is an important perspective, why don't we reference it?*

- *I've learned from autistic people that the community mostly prefers a gold or rainbow infinity symbol. Blue puzzle pieces are controversial and cause distress for many autistic people.*

- *I know that the usual approach fits into the system better, but I'd like to try this other way, because the autistic community has been advocating to change that.*

To be clear, I'm not proposing to change any verbiage. Claiming allyship isn't a hill I'd die on. But you will never hear me refer to myself as an ally of any group, because I don't feel like it's up to me to make that decision. A person's allyship is fluid and can change in a heartbeat. As you've probably concluded from my previous chapters, most autistic advocates would have called me a threat to their community just a few years ago.

Key Points

- As parents advocate for their children, we should take the lead from the autistic community. Oftentimes, we have a lot of learning and unlearning to do, and that's okay!

- Autistic parents have a unique perspective, yet they are often ostracized from parent-led spaces, including advocacy forums. Allistic parents should ensure that autistic parents are respected, and that their voices are heard.

- When parents use respectful language, we set a precedence for others to follow. We can advocate for services and support without dehumanizing autistic people.

Resources to Explore

Leaders around Me edited by Edlyn Peña Ph.D.

Typed Words Loud Voices edited by Amy Sequenzia and Elizabeth J. Grace

The Edge of the Playground by Mikhaela Ackerman and Mary Lynn Ackerman Willis

This Is Not About Me, a film featuring nonspeaking advocate Jordyn Zimmerman

   https://thisisnotaboutme.film

LET'S GET TO WORK

Tee Mone't

I am autistic/ADHD and my mind zeroes in on things.

So if I'm sitting in a chair and talking to someone at a party, the only way to focus on our conversation is for everything else happening around us to disappear.

I can't focus on the entire picture happening around me, it'd be like trying to focus on a bunch of multicolored objects flying around at warp speed and trying to pick out the various colors splattered onto each one.

If I focus too intently on even what's going on in our corner, I can feel my clothes, the chair, voices start blending into one; if I look at their face it will warp and change.

This is where stimming comes in, to disperse the attention evenly so I don't get overwhelmed by one sensation.

The problem is that sensory overload causes me to lose all spatial and body awareness, so I can't effectively stim away the pressure, which means I will explode.

Transitions are hard because shutting and opening a door, going into a different room, is to enter a different world. With a different temperature and different people and a different atmosphere. It can be instant calm, or instant dysregulation. The people here can look friendly, or like a threat.

It is better to look directly at absolutely nothing in this state, lest I not be able to break away. All of my stuffed animals have closed or not very detailed eyes, and I don't keep posters of real people on my walls. Sensory overload can make things that usually bring you happiness seem sinister.

Everything is a trip for me. And my mood, how regulated I am, how safe I feel, affects the experience. The way I experience the world is always different from someone who isn't autistic. But these factors affect if I interpret the experience as good or bad. The intensity of negative experiences affects how soon I'll try things again.

I've noticed two ways autistic people tend to internalize this reality: by worrying intensely about how other people will react if we lose control, or focusing intently on losing control.

I have become the latter.

I don't care how people react to my constant pacing and swaying. I know if I stand still the walls will start closing in. And when that happens, any other sensation, even pain, can keep my mind off of that feeling. Bring me back to earth.

I am no longer bothered as much by what people think but bothered by feeling so awful during and after a meltdown and bothered about someone being caught in the crossfire.

And I find this better because I am actually the only person I can depend on.

So I'm gonna give you my personal reasoning for why I really don't like when people film autistic kids or put things out there just because "they don't understand anyway."

My life is a series of delayed processing. Things I didn't respond to the first time hit me like a freight train a couple days, even weeks later; my thoughts are not linear.

Sometimes I really don't understand what is happening.

That's why to some people I seem fearless. I'm not fearless, I literally cannot process the element of danger.

I didn't just "not care what anyone thinks." I didn't understand that the way people think can actually affect you, until much later in life when I tried to apply for jobs or make relationships.

If I understood that those girls were actually making fun of me in the third grade, I would have cared.

I would have stopped trying to be friends with them.

No one wants to be made fun of. No one wants people to allow things to happen just because we "don't understand anyway."

CHAPTER THIRTEEN

Productive Conflict

—— JULES ——

I'm a bit of an idealist. I'm enthusiastic about coaxing the world to be a better place for everyone. I can't accept the way the world is, because it's such a messed-up place for so many people, for so many reasons. There are other people who subscribe to the idea that "the real world is not going to accommodate you, you'll need to just deal with it." I think that statement is completely false.

As I've said, now is not a time for blind trust. It's not a time for hand holding or toxic positivity. There will always be conflict, as long as our community is being abused, segregated, and worse. For those who want to make life better for autistic people, this is a time for productive conflict. We need non-autistic people to hear us, to learn from us, to boost our messages. We need more bridge builders.

My suggestions for allistic parents throughout this book are meant to help guide them towards learning from autistic people, even when it's hard. Understanding where autistic people are coming from and learning from their perspectives will help parents advocate for their children more effectively, both today and in preparation for their children's tomorrow.

My suggestions for autistic people are not meant to convince autistic people how they should or shouldn't interact with allistic parents, but rather to share some ideas I've learned along the way about how to be more effective in reaching them.

A value of the Anishinaabe culture, one of the 7 Grandfather

Teachings, is "Humble yourself to your fellow human in the way you walk with him or her." My work as an Indigenous autistic woman is my contribution to the community, it's my way of walking alongside others in their journey.

Is This a Hill You'd Die On?

I don't want to die on every hill. I've found it to be counterproductive. While I feel passionate about many topics, I don't have an unlimited pool of energy. For any number of reasons, I may choose to walk away from a conversation or conflict. We each need to decide how to expend our energy. If we don't set limits, there will be an unlimited demand for our time and energy.

I've learned that focusing on the bigger picture is a better use of my time. While I want a more perfect world, I can also accept and celebrate progress. As I mentioned in Chapter Two, intersectionality, racial equity, and communication rights are hills I'm prepared to die on. What are your passions? What are your strengths? What do you *not* like to do or talk about? Flow charts and bubble maps can be helpful in working out which topics are worth spending energy on, and which aren't as pertinent.

Planting Seeds

As an enthusiastic brown-thumb gardener, I've learned that sometimes all I can do is plant seeds. The seed's environment does more to determine whether that seed sprouts and blooms or if the seed degrades underground. Is the seed being watered enough, but not too much? Is the soil too acidic? Does it have enough nutrients? Does the seedling have the right amount of sun? Are there pollinators, to help pollinate the seedlings and grow fruit?

Different seeds have different germination rates. Not every seed is able to sprout. If we think of an idea as a metaphorical seed, we'd think about all of the different environmental factors that impact whether or not that idea can sprout and blossom.

Not all ideas will come to fruition, because not every idea will have the proper environment in which to grow.

Sometimes, when an autistic advocate is trying to reach a parent with a new idea, it may be the first time that parent has heard this new idea. That new idea may be combating systemic ableism and years of conditioning that society and medical systems have ingrained in the parent's mind. That first seed may not grow, but maybe a seed with a low germination rate needs a hundred attempts in order for one of them to grow. You won't reach everyone you try to reach.

Sometimes all you can do is plant a seed.

Taking Care of Ourselves

Autistic advocacy is frustrating and overwhelming at times, and it is work, and it is okay to take breaks as long and as frequently as needed. The idea that we must always be working on something is a product of capitalism, which is inherently ableist. Your worth doesn't depend on your productivity.

Self-care isn't only bubble baths and facial masks. Self-care is also recognizing when your emotional health, physical health, and overall wellness needs attention. Self-care can include therapy and finding balance in your life. Self-care is loving yourself enough to protect yourself from harmful situations. Self-care is walking away from things that are bringing you more pain than joy. Self-care is learning about sensory and emotional regulation. Self-care is working on addressing your own trauma to develop healthy coping mechanisms.

You are in control of your own engagement. If you need to take a break from advocacy work, whether it is local grassroots advocacy, boards or workgroups, or social media, please take a break! If you need to unfollow autism groups so that you can enjoy your social media experience, and only engage with conversations about autism when you make the active choice to engage, it may help you compartmentalize your interactions.

While our personal lives require advocacy, advocacy doesn't

require us to always be "on" to perform service to others. Always being available for advocacy work is a quick route to burnout. Emotional labor is labor. Advocacy work is work. And you do not owe anyone any kind of one-on-one engagement. If you do not have the energy to hold a conversation, but you do want to provide information, make it as easy as possible on yourself.

Scripting (reciting words or phrases) is often an autistic strength. Leverage this to conserve your own energy. If you say or write a response to a topic that could be used in other contexts, make a mental, physical, or digital note, and use it as a script in the future. Write a blanket response about topics that you regularly address and save it in your cloud drive or email or somewhere else so that you can copy and paste it. It's not cheating, I promise.

When you don't want to go back and forth with a parent, but you have information you'd like to share, keep a bookmark folder with links to research, articles, blogs, etc. that align with your perspective. Drop the link and turn off notifications.

There are a few key communication techniques that allistic people respond well to and make them more receptive to constructive criticism, which you can use if and when you choose to:

- Validate feelings and provide additional information. Sometimes, even when a person's feelings are based on lack of information or misperceptions, they just want their feelings to be validated. An example of this could be:

  It seems like you're feeling really worried that your child will only eat one thing, and you just want to make sure they're getting all of the nutrition that they need. Have you ever heard about samefood? Here's an article I've found helpful.

- Sandwich constructive criticism between encouragement. This way, parents don't feel personally attacked. An example could be:

  Wow, that's a really fun activity that you're planning

to do together! You mentioned your child has sensory sensitivities—maybe the sensory-friendly show would be a better option than making them go to the busy show. Desensitization doesn't really work when it comes to sensory sensitivities. I love how you're so enthusiastic about your child being able to see Elmo because he loves Elmo so much.

Sometimes, overlooking the "wrong" part to provide a better alternative is more well received than outright saying, "This is harmful and here's why." Many parents are open to learning, but they struggle to get past hearing that they're wrong about something. This is not exclusive to allistics, autistics have the same reaction at times. Using positive language—"Do this"—rather than negative language—"Don't do that"—helps get past this barrier.

- *Yes, and...* Derived from improv, this is a great way to both validate what another person is saying, while providing additional context or perspective. When we say *"But..."* people perceive it as invalidation and argument, even if you only mean to provide additional information. It takes practice to use this strategy *and* it makes a huge difference when talking about sensitive topics.

Attack ideas, not people. When people feel attacked, they can't learn. This concept felt so wrong when I first came across it. If someone says or does something harmful, I felt like they should be open to learning how to do better. But if the person is feeling like they're being accused of doing something wrong, particularly when they think they're doing something right, they may be defensive and unwilling to listen to how their mistake has hurt others. Attacking ideas instead of people is a matter of nuance, and it has been a valuable skill for me to learn. For instance, instead of telling parents they're disrespecting or harming their children, I can direct my attention to the specific words or actions.

No matter how well-intentioned your feedback, there will always be people who become defensive or lash out in response. We can't own how people receive the information that we give them, and we can't own what others do with the information we give them. That can be a difficult thought to cope with, but it's also an illustration of the importance of developing boundaries.

Setting, Enforcing, and Experiencing Boundaries

Boundaries are an important part of protecting ourselves from harm. Protecting ourselves isn't often an autistic strength. We are often too trusting, too willing to help others at our own expense, and too forgiving.

Setting and enforcing boundaries is an important part of self-preservation. It sets limits to interpersonal relationships. It is a means to exert self-control, defining what we will and won't engage in, and communicating those decisions with others. Boundaries are often misunderstood. Sometimes, people misuse the word "boundaries" when they are trying to control the actions of others:

- *An example of a boundary*: I won't go to this event because it doesn't feel safe to me.

- *Not an example of a boundary*: You should not go to this event, because it doesn't feel safe to me.

Sometimes, people who experience other people's boundaries don't react well. They may get upset or they may try to convince you to do things that you are uncomfortable with. Their feelings are their responsibility, and it is not our responsibility to comfort them.

Sometimes, when people set boundaries with us, it can feel like rejection. That person is setting boundaries because they are practicing self-care, not because they are rejecting us as a person.

We need to cope with those feelings of rejection, without trying to change the other person's mind.

Here are some examples of boundaries:

- *Set and communicate a schedule for yourself.* Only respond to advocacy-related calls and messages during the time you have reserved, and only if your mind and heart are in a space that is healthy for you. One app that can help is you can book me (https://youcanbook.me).

- *Set limitations regarding topics that make you uncomfortable.* Let the people around you know that it is something you're unwilling to discuss, or if you'd like other people to ask you if it's okay to talk about the uncomfortable topic.

When in Crisis

Autistics, when you are in crisis, please exercise self-care and do not subject yourself to hostile spaces where you feel the need to justify your existence and you're subjected to bigotry. Sometimes, autism advocacy is a form of self-harm. Walk away, take leave, unfollow, take care of you until you're ready to re-engage. The community has your back, we will continue the fight while you take care of you. Self-care is a radical act under the colonial-capitalist system that we live in. You need to take care of yourself because, oftentimes, you're the only one who will.

During the course of your advocacy, you will encounter parents in crisis, and parents whose autistic children are in crisis. I see it over and over again: parents whose families are in crisis are attacked for using the wrong language, the wrong symbols, expressing ableist ideas. There is a time and a place to engage in this conversation, but it is not when children's safety is at risk.

Sometimes, we autistics can't see the forest for the trees. This is an idiom that means that there is a very large issue that needs immediate attention, but we're focused on details that aren't relevant at the moment.

Parents in crisis are desperate for help, and when they come to ask autistic people for help—as we always suggest they do— they may be corrected for mistakes, rather than helped with what they asked for. If we can set aside those conversations during a crisis, and we can make a meaningful impact on an autistic child's life and their parent's life, that parent is going to be more open to learning about those finer details when they're out of crisis.

We also need to recognize the very real risk that a child experiencing a crisis may be at heightened risk of abuse or filicide. If we can help the parent de-escalate and problem solve, the safer that child is. If their metaphorical forest is on fire, they can't stop to look at each individual tree. Help them put out the fire first if you can. And if you can't, please don't light another match.

A Gentle Call-in on Errorless Autism Advocacy

When I learned of my autism diagnosis, I fell into a pattern of trying to find "the right way" to be autistic. I wanted to do everything right, fit into what I was supposed to think, feel, say, and do, because I thought I finally found a place of belonging. I lost myself while searching for community, and I wasn't making choices that aligned with my personal or cultural values. I wasn't interacting with others in a good way. I got swept away.

Some people feel a lot of pride in their identity. Some people feel really lost and overwhelmed and wish they weren't autistic. And far too often, I see autistic people shamed for expressing feelings that may be a result of trauma. The difficult feelings that autistic people experience are valid, and they're often rooted in bullying, oppression, discrimination, and abuse.

Instead of validating and supporting autistics who are struggling, some spaces in our community shame them for expressing those feelings. That's not something I can support. I want to welcome autistic people with open arms and reassure them that they belong and provide comfort and space for healing from a lifetime of rejection and trauma.

No one warns autistic advocates what they're signing up for. It can be ugly. Autistic advocacy is brutal, in part because autistic people are treated brutally by society, and in part because we aren't always kind to one another.

There are rules in some autistic spaces that violate what I know about disability justice. There are demands to disclose one's diagnosis, use prescribed language, and conform to predetermined rules. Sometimes the rules are 30-page documents! And autistic people are expected to follow the predetermined rules that they had no say in creating, without support. If these rules are broken, there are harsh consequences.

Strict rules about language and behavior are kind of antithetic to the idea of self-determination. Shouldn't we be supporting autistic people to learn, rather than bullying them when they don't already know what we know, or believe what we believe?

I learned from Lydia X.Z. Brown that person-first language was introduced by people with intellectual disabilities (ID), in response to the routine dehumanization of people with ID. And these days, autistic people with ID are straight up bullied for saying they're a "person with a disability" or "person with autism" or "person with intellectual disability."

For what? Who does that serve? While I choose to identify myself as an autistic person, someone who chooses to identify as a person with autism isn't causing me harm. Other autistic people aren't the enemy. It is our job as a community to model how we want the rest of the world to treat us. If we want society to support us, we need to support one another. If we want society to include us, we need to include one another.

When other autistic people are engaging in problematic autism advocacy, it is our job as a community to collect our own people and provide support so they can learn. When an autistic person is being ableist, we need to help them understand why it's problematic. When a white autistic person is being racist, we need other white autistics to help them understand why it's problematic.

We need to extend patience and grace with one another. We need to understand that internalized ableism is a symptom of autistic people being victims of ableism. Internalizing the discrimination that they've experienced is a survival mechanism. Further, people with co-occurring learning or intellectual disabilities may need one-on-one support to unlearn ableism. And they have a right to support from the community, not ostracization. I'm not going to get everything right. Neither will you.

As a parent, I understand the value of advocating for the support that each of my children needs. Having to participate in the special education process for three disabled children with very different support needs, having to advocate for different things for each child, I understand how every autistic person is different and needs different supports. And I wholeheartedly believe that every autistic person has a right to the supports that they need.

Disability justice must not be based on lateral violence and the refusal to support those in our community who need support to learn and embrace new ideas. Disability justice must not include attacking and rejecting disabled people who are still learning about disability justice. Disability justice must not perpetuate white supremacy, lashing out at those most marginalized in favor of the rules that white autistics adopt and enforce. Gatekeeping access to the autistic community isn't disability justice.

And this is a hill I would die on.

Imperfect Resources

Upon my children's diagnoses, I felt driven to learn everything that I could. I borrowed every book, woefully too few, from the local library system. I watched videos, I read blogs. I didn't have an agenda other than learning about autism so that I could be a better parent, because I felt like a failure.

The first book I read was *Uniquely Human*, written by Barry Prizant (2015). It was written from an allistic perspective, yet it still helped me better understand my children, and it was one of the more accessible books available. At the time, it was eye-opening, and helped me understand autism in the context of being the caregiver of an autistic person. Reading this book led me to look for autistic perspectives.

While there is some valid criticism of *Uniquely Human*, it serves a purpose in the broader autism discourse, and it was a good starting point for me, given where my understanding of autism began. At the time of writing, an updated edition of *Uniquely Human* is soon to be published.

It's helpful when autism resources adapt over time, as language and our understanding evolve. One example is the original *Females and Autism/Aspergers: A Checklist* by Samantha Craft. At the time I read it, it was incredibly helpful for me. The language used in the original resource became outdated due to the gendered language and use of the term "Aspergers," and she later revised the resource to become *Samantha Craft's Autistic Traits Checklist* (Craft 2020).

A work being imperfect or becoming antiquated doesn't mean that the work is useless; it means that we continue to learn new information over time, and we need to build on prior information to continue learning. We need imperfect resources because people are imperfect. Imperfect resources serve a purpose.

Not everyone has the same experiences and understanding, and many of us have internalized harmful rhetoric about what it means to be autistic and what we're supposed to do about it. Sometimes a gentle introduction to new concepts can be more effective than a bold statement that everything we know is wrong.

We have to meet people where they are, not where we think they should be. I didn't know about language preferences or the historical and current perspectives about cause, intervention, treatment, and support, so I didn't read this information through a critical lens at the time. I needed time to learn, just as we all do. Many parents of autistic children are autistic themselves, and most don't know. Not being diagnosed doesn't negate the need for support to learn.

Cultural Competency

Matthew Rushin, a young Black autistic man, was arrested after a vehicle accident in 2019. He was taken to jail without medical treatment and interrogated without the police following proper protocols. His mother reached out for help on social media, sharing a digital flyer with his face on it, and a puzzle-piece ribbon.

Meghan is local to Matthew and shared the mother's post to her blog. Soon after, she reached out to me for guidance. The autistic community wasn't happy that she shared the image, due to the controversial history of the puzzle piece. As a non-autistic parent and as a white person, she knew it wasn't her place to correct anyone or tell anyone how they should feel. She also knew that Matthew needed help, and she used her page to boost visibility.

The response from white autistics about that post was a turning point for me. To see dozens of white autistics more upset that a Black mother used a puzzle piece, with complete disregard for the fact that a young autistic Black man was in a jail cell, with his life at risk... It changed my perception of the autistic community entirely.

It isn't just Matthew Rushin.

It's also Darius McCollum, a Black autistic man whose fascination with trains has caused him to be criminalized. Whereas white autistic men who have demonstrated the same passion about trains have been rewarded with training, jobs, and celebration, Darius is sitting in a jail cell with a neglected year-old Change.org petition because the white autistic community doesn't show up in force to support Black autistics. The petition has been ignored because of language that has been perceived to be problematic by the white autistic community.

It's also Joshua Nixon, an Indigenous man who was a victim of police brutality while walking home from work. The abuse he suffered was ignored because Indigenous erasure happens in the autistic community as well.

It's all of the autistic women, trans, and nonbinary people of color who will never be able to access a diagnosis, treatment, or support because of their race and gender identity.

It's all of the young Black and Indigenous autistic children who are removed from their parents' care because the family is struggling. No support or services are offered to the family.

Those children are often placed in white foster homes and court-ordered to participate in full-time ABA. The autistic community generally agrees that ABA is an abusive practice, yet most of the energy is spent on shaming frightened parents rather than ending institutional practices that target children of color.

To white people... It is not your place to "correct" people of color in the greater autism community. No, not even if whatever exception you're trying to think of happens. Not your place. Do not scold, chastise, or dogpile allistic parents of color or autistics of color. The people leading the conversation about ableism in communities of color are autistic people of color, and it is the role of white autistics to support autistic people of color.

Even when the language or symbols are not preferred, we still need to show up and work towards liberation of those autistics who are most marginalized by racist and ableist systems. To ignore autistic people of color sitting in jail cells because their family or friends use non-preferred language in a petition is to be complicit with institutionalized racism.

The same is true for people of different cultures. Too many times, I've witnessed parents of autistic children dogpiled and kicked out of learning spaces because they don't use the language that white autistics prefer. Or they are shamed for their cultural perceptions of autism and disability.

Recently, a parent in one autistic-led learning group asked for advice on how to gently educate her husband, to protect her son from enduring a provider-recommended 40 hours of ABA every week. She specifically stated that she was from a culture which valued the decisions of husbands and not those of wives. One person after another advised her to "leave him." The comments made by people who actually answered her question were deleted, accused of being pro-ABA, while the comments were actually meant to help her navigate the circumstances with a focus on harm reduction for her entire family, including her child.

CHAPTER FOURTEEN

In Autistic Space

—— MEGHAN ——

There's a key point about allyship that I'd like to highlight in this chapter: The people who seek to support a marginalized community shouldn't expect free labor from that marginalized community. This includes emotional labor, physical labor, and time. While physical labor is self-explanatory, emotional labor and time seem to cause more confusion. As a general rule, those who aren't members of a marginalized community should complete their own homework and make the effort to learn the history and key issues within the community from the resources already available.

As parents of autistic children, we're fortunate to have spaces dedicated to helping us learn the things we would otherwise have to research for on our own. Due to the decades-long misinformation campaign and ongoing abuse fueled by mega corporations, this particular community doesn't have much of a choice but to intervene.

This does not mean, however, that we should take their collaboration for granted and abuse this additional privilege we've been afforded. If you're thinking about joining a few of these groups, which I would recommend if you're thinking about advocating in some form, allow me to share what I've learned from my own journey.

For Parents New to Autistic-Led Learning...

1. Remember your purpose

I entered autistic-led forums for one reason, and that was for my children. I wanted to gain a better understanding of what they were experiencing and how I could best support them. Autistic adults are in these forums for the same reason, for *our* children. They want to help *us* gain this understanding because they know how much misinformation we're being fed. Autistic adults were once autistic children. They grew up in our school systems. They know first-hand what changes society needs to make in order to become more accessible and inclusive.

There are days when emotions run high in these groups and it's easy to lose sight of that goal. When I'm scrolling on social media, autism posts are scattered between funny memes and political hostility. I try to remain mindful of this, and only interact when I'm in the headspace to absorb and reflect.

2. Listen first, second, and third. Speak last

Advocacy work requires much more input than output, especially in the beginning. The autistic community has been talked over, mistreated, and undervalued their entire lives. For that very reason, autistic-led groups are run much differently than typical parent-led forums. It's important to understand the culture and rules each group has developed before we start interacting.

I'm in several autistic-led forums where parents can ask a question and receive feedback from dozens of autistic adults, instantly. These volunteers choose to provide emotional labor and time for the sake of our kids. But frustrations arise when parents ask the same questions over and over again. As a parent, I understand that we come in with specific questions and want them answered immediately. But as a longtime member of those groups, I also understand how upsetting it is to see the same question asked over and over again.

Pay attention to which forum you're in. Each group has a unique vibe depending on its focus. Take a few weeks to read the posts, responses, topics, and rules. Some of them have rules that restrict responses to a certain group for a specific period of time. Others don't allow non-autistic parents to respond to certain posts. Many group leaders have taken the extra step to develop reading lists and FAQs. These resources can help bring newcomers up to speed and cut down the labor autistic members spend answering the same questions day after day. Take advantage!

3. Get comfortable with being uncomfortable
When we enter autistic space, we should do so with respect and check our egos at the door. It's natural for parents to feel defensive when our views are challenged, especially when it comes to raising our children. *We're* accustomed to being experts on that topic. And while it's true that nobody knows our children better than we do, we aren't experts on living autistically unless we are autistic ourselves.

I once posted a picture of the twins dying eggs during April. I was concerned that Nick was stressed because he was fisting and didn't smile the entire time. I insisted that this wasn't a forced activity and asked the group what they thought the problem was. The first few responses were all the same.

"Why do they *have* to smile?"

Huh? Because they're having a good time? I didn't say that because I was obviously missing something. Then other members chimed in.

"Honestly, people judging me and getting mad about my facial expressions as a child was deeply unpleasant and made me feel broken. I know you're worried about their emotional health, but one of the best ways to do this is to let them be themselves."

After I reflected a bit, it made perfect sense. I don't smile when I'm concentrating, but that doesn't mean I'm not enjoying myself. When I smile at people, I usually make that smile for them. By expecting them to smile, I was inadvertently encouraging them to mask for me. Masking is suppressing your natural way of being and acting in a way that someone else expects.

Keep in mind that the autistic community isn't a homogeneous group. Each person's lived experience is as different as yours and mine. There will be times the advice we're given doesn't apply to our own children. Instead of challenging the merits of the person offering advice, trust their testimony. While it may not apply to your children, there are plenty of other parents in the room who may find those particular insights useful.

4. Don't assume intent

One of the responders to my egg-dying question said, "Don't expect people to smile all the time." There are a few different ways I could take that comment. My instinct would be to process this statement as an attack and respond in kind. I've done that more than a few times over the years and it got me nowhere. I only ended up insulting the person who took the time to educate me and derailing the entire conversation. Another way to view this comment, which I've learned to be most helpful, is at face value.

"Don't expect people to smile all the time."

Good point. Got it.

In this scenario, there were enough other responses for me to understand the context. That's one great part about these groups—lots of perspectives. If his response was the only one, I would've asked him to explain a little more if he had the time and energy.

During any interaction in autistic-led online forums, there could be several communication barriers to overcome. Obviously there's a difference between autistic and neurotypical communication. But more than that, we can't hear intonation or see facial expressions when we're on the computer. Even if we could, autistic tone and facial expressions may not match what neurotypical people are expecting. The egg-dying story is a great example of that.

Don't assume hostility, especially over the computer. I can't count the number of times I see parents say, "Why are you so mad?" While some people may be better at sugar-coating information, others communicate more directly. Oftentimes the person talking to us may speak a different native language than we do. Our goal isn't to get information in a gentle way. It's simply to get the information.

We should be patient and responsive to autistic mentors if they have follow-up questions. They get asked the same questions multiple times a day from parents who have not taken the time to read through previously answered posts or questions. If someone asks if you've read the group's announcements or FAQs provided, take that question at face value, and remember, it's our job to do our homework.

5. Take your time

It all seemed so urgent in the beginning. I felt like I was failing as a parent if I didn't do all-of-the-things right away. My heart beats a little faster when I think back to that period of time—the overscheduling, the waiting lists, the panic. The idea of catching up, the claim that there's a small window of opportunity, the insistence of filling out milestone charts at every appointment— it's all trash. I wish I could get that time back. I'd spend it at the playground, or the beach, or *anywhere* besides an appointment.

Jules' AutismMoon suggests that parents take the entire year following our children's autism diagnosis to actively do nothing about it—no therapies, and no rushing. Unless there's a crisis or medical issue, we should simply enjoy our children and take that time to learn more about autism from the people who've been in our children's shoes.

With that sentiment in mind, don't overwhelm yourself or your kids. If the back-and-forth dialogue of learning forums gets to be too much, books are a wonderful way to learn. Lots of them have audio versions if that's your preferred way to read. Take breaks when you feel stressed. I'm talking about blackout breaks. There are times when I spend days binge watching my favorite show with the phone on silent. No information coming in, or out.

6. Bring others along on your journey

I placed this down at #6 for a reason. I've learned a lot since I started my blog—the main point being I started it too quickly (see tip #2). While my intentions were good, wanting to bring other parents along as I learned, I didn't fully grasp the impact my words could have. When we engage with the mainstream community, our main goal should be to amplify the message of autistic people themselves. We can't know what those messages are without taking our time to listen and learn.

Autistic advocates have their hands full—educating parents, transforming the medical field, and welcoming adults who are new to their own neurodivergence. It's important for us to look at what autistic advocates are trying to do and help take those projects on. Non-autistic parents may have fewer executive functioning issues, fewer co-occurring conditions, better access to words, and familiarity speaking the allistic language.

In order to make a greater impact, it's important to involve people who aren't directly connected with the autism community—business owners, community leaders, clubs and leagues, fraternities, and sororities. The more people with skin in the game, the greater change we can effect. Obviously, I'm not suggesting that individual people should reach out to all of those communities. But if each of us reached out to one or two outside groups, the impact would be tremendous. I'm a former public-school teacher, so I tend to focus on that community. Progress surrounding inclusion and compassionate practices is being hindered due to lack of teacher training and misinformation.

During the first summer of Covid, I facilitated two month-long *Unprofessional Developments* for educators, administrators, parents, and of course autistic advocates. To be clear, I don't have a bunch of letters behind my name. But what I do have is a community that I've been building, a network of people who know a lot more stuff than I do, who are passionate about changing the world. That summer, my community grew exponentially! We spent the entire month using *Beyond Behaviors* by Dr. Mona Delahooke to fuel meaningful discussions surrounding inclusion, compassionate teaching, restraint and seclusion, intersectionality, all-of-the-things. We hosted guest speakers, held over a hundred Zoom chats, and ended that summer feeling more connected and empowered than when we started.

Six months later I splintered off with one of my Unprofessional

Developers. Dr. Maisha Otway, a principal in Fulton County, Georgia, wanted to improve the culture of her own school, so she invited me to a semester-long book study with her work family. That experience was inspiring in a completely different way. We spent the whole semester, through pandemic lockdowns and political shenanigans, talking about real-life concerns and brainstorming real-life solutions for their specific school. Now that's world changing.

7. Be prepared for friction

Once I started unpacking my own ableism, I began to share what I was learning. It's not that I subscribed to the tragedy narrative in the first place, but the moment I started actively challenging it, all hell broke loose. All of a sudden it wasn't Jules calling me names, it was my fellow parents.

Going against the status quo doesn't make anyone wildly popular. It's the tragedy narrative that sells, remember? If I wanted to gain followers and be the popular parent on the block, I could get in my car each week and record myself crying, or I could write about how my heart sinks when I glance over at my kid playing alone at the park. If my goal was to get sponsors, I could post Instagram pictures promoting the latest vitamin masquerading as an autism supplement.

One of my articles challenged the grief narrative surrounding our autistic children's diagnosis. In my article, I was careful not to invalidate what parents were feeling. My argument was that we as parents could use more specific words to describe those feelings. Almost immediately, another parent blogger who I had never even heard of started mocking me on her page. She read my article and thought I was referencing a speech she gave about grieving for her own child. *I mean if the shoe fits…*

Honestly, none of these topics come without conflict. But I'm passionate about helping parents and educators who are still open to learning, and I can't do that if I'm constantly fighting the people who I know full well are baiting me. New parents who are simply watching and absorbing won't understand the context. They'll just see me as a bully. Whenever that type of hostility arises, I try to remain calm and remember that I'm not necessarily speaking to the person who's calling me names or assassinating my character. I'm speaking to the audience.

I remember myself in the beginning, with zero knowledge about autism. I want to reach them before they go to the cures and misery pages. I want to give them resources and hope. I want to show them how wonderful and different neurodiversity is. That's my goal. I'm speaking to the person who's never typed a word. That's the person who's absorbing the information, learning about AAC devices, and changing their own attitude about the children.

8. Focus on interests instead of positions

There's an old story my mom told me about two children who wanted an orange. Both of them *insisted* that they needed the entire orange, but there was only one left. So the mom did what most moms would do in that situation—cut it in the middle and gave them each half. The first child squeezed the juice out of his half to make orange juice. The second child used the peel of the orange to make muffins. As it turned out, they each could have gotten the entire part of the orange that they desired, or the whole amount that they needed, if they had communicated a little more.

This strategy comes from the field of mediation, and focuses on highlighting our concerns rather than our positions. It is particularly helpful with explosive debates. We all have different perspectives and live with different circumstances. If our goal is to change this world and make it better for our children, and if we choose to take part in the more difficult work of building bridges, we first have to realize that there's always more to the conversation than just *our* positions. When we draw lines in the sand, nothing much gets accomplished. But if we can push through our own egos, figure out our common interests, we can use those to at least move in a better direction.

9. Use I-statements

When trouble arises, and it always does, remember that not all trouble is bad. Growth only happens when we wander outside of our comfort zone. Stay cool and remember you're always talking to the audience. To be fair, my mom has to remind me about this all the time. I should've named this chapter *Barb's Advice*.

Instead of telling people what *they* should do or how *they* sound, I *try* to tell people what I do, or how I feel. (*See what I just did there?*) This is an especially great tool for topics that make people instantly defensive.

Example One:

- Stop using the puzzle piece. That's ableist.

- When I see a puzzle piece, I want to scream. Here's an article about why the autistic community uses the infinity instead.

Example Two:

- Stop using person-first language. That's ableist.

- Realizing my kids were autistic as opposed to *having* autism, it was a game changer for me. Here are a few articles that helped me understand that.

Example Three:

- That book is trash. You shouldn't read it.

- I didn't like that book because it talks about autism treatments instead of support. Here are a few the autistic community recommends on the same topic.

I realize that the second response in each example requires more effort than the first. And we don't always have the time and energy to engage on that level. But if we choose to take part in the more difficult work of building bridges, this is an approach I've found useful. When I don't have the energy, I can always tag a friend like we're in a WWF match, or simply write BRB (be right back) so I remember to come back to it later (see #5).

As parents navigating autistic space, we're going to have missteps and blunders. There's no doubt about it. Nobody's perfect and we all bring our own baggage to the table. I'll be the first to admit that I've made plenty of decisions that I wish I could take back—both with my kids and with the adult autistic community as a whole. But when we keep our purpose in mind and remain open to learning, we can help this community (of which our children are the tiniest members) influence meaningful change.

Grace...

It's been over four years since I first dipped my toes into the world of autism and I've been completely submerged ever since. This passion has become my career and I have the coolest job in the world. I can transition from taking a course to presenting at a conference, from interviewing an autistic author to facilitating a school-wide book study, all in the same week! There's nothing I'd rather do than help accelerate this paradigm shift, away from the old-school medical model and toward the more accessible and inclusive social model.

As we keep pushing forward with our own learning, it's easy to forget that each day parents around the world are starting from square one. They're sitting in the doctor's office listening to the same narrative I was told—the severity levels, the mental age, the medical model. They've never heard of AAC devices or received guidance on using visuals. These parents are joining groups with other parents who are equally unknowledgeable.

For many parents who find my website or social media channels, it's their first introduction to the idea that they don't need to be sad about their children being autistic, and that their children don't need to be fixed. It's not that my content is better than others, but I'm in the *parenting niche*, and it's natural for parents to look to other parents for advice in the beginning.

In many online forums, including my own, I see these new

parents being criticized for using the pathologizing language they've been taught. They're being harshly judged for sharing their feelings of anxiety and fear. Instead of being welcomed, they're ostracized—even by parents who once shared those same views. While this section seems to contradict a lot of what I talk about in the book, it's merely a reminder that we should treat people the way we would have wanted people to treat us in the beginning.

Even I am guilty of losing my temper occasionally—I'm not the most serene person you'll ever meet. When my mom and I chat, she'll often interrupt me using her calm voice... "Green, Meghan. Stay green." (If you have ever read *Beyond Behaviors*, this should make you chuckle.)

One time, without thinking, I entered an online discussion when I saw a parent ask, "Why can't we all just get along?" She was talking about autistic advocates and parents. My fingers apparently had a mind of their own that evening and typed out, "Pick a side, already. It's not that complicated!"

That wasn't one of my finest moments.

It's easy to become unforgiving toward those who don't use the latest terminology. It's easy to forget that just because *we* know something, that doesn't necessarily make it common knowledge. It's easy to belittle those parents who aren't at the same levels of knowledge and acceptance as we are.

It takes more effort to meet our fellow parents where they are and empathize with how they're feeling—and that's exactly what we should do. As parents continue on their learning journey, they'll hopefully learn to unpack what they brought into diagnosis day and all of the misinformation that they received shortly after. But none of that learning and unpacking will happen if we don't remain compassionate to newcomers.

Key Points

- Allistic parents should enter autistic spaces with the goal of listening, learning, and absorbing. Autistic people mentor parents to protect autistic children, not to protect our feelings.

- Autism resources become antiquated over time because our understanding of autism and the language we use changes. It's best to find up-to-date resources that are recommended by the autistic community.

- It may take time for parents to unlearn what they've been taught. As autistic advocates, we should take care of ourselves. Remember that the seeds we plant take time to grow.

- We should treat each other with respect and patience. We should treat ourselves the same way.

Resources to Explore

"Samantha Craft's Autistic Traits Checklist"

www.myspectrumsuite.com/samantha-crafts-autistic-traits-checklist

Uniquely Human. Updated and expanded by Barry Prizant

Online courses for parents and educators:

Foundations for Divergent Minds Training

www.divergentminds.org

InTune Families with Kristy Forbes

www.kristyforbes.com.au

The Inside of Autism with Kieran Rose

https://theautisticadvocate.com/onlinelearning

Aucademy Trainings

https://aucademy.co.uk

WHERE DO I FIT IN?

CHAPTER FIFTEEN

Finding My Niche

— JULES AND MEGHAN —

O ur goal is to make the world a better place for all autistics, present and future.

There's power in numbers. Substantial change takes working together, and that's not always easy with a large group, especially when the group is made up of people with varying knowledge, experiences, and goals. Especially when some group members are members of a privileged class, and others are members of an oppressed class. Intersectionality applies here.

Being autistic or being the parent of an autistic person means that we have to advocate. Whether we are engaging in self-advocacy, advocacy for our child, or policy advocacy, it is an integral part of the autistic and caregiving experience. There are so many opportunities for advocacy and community involvement, some of which are occasional activities and others are long-term commitments.

Each person has to decide for themselves what kind of energy and time they have available. Each person can evaluate their own interests, passions, strengths, and areas of need. Bring a friend with you to increase engagement or for support. Seek out those who are open to learning and motivated to change the world.

Opportunities

If you don't know where to begin, this chapter will include a variety of ideas for getting involved. We know that people care about issues but may not know where to start.

Informal and Grassroots Involvement

- Develop a local community. Be inclusive of people you are trying to reach. Lots of people have a need for support to learn new concepts. Don't expect everyone else to know what you know.

- Sign up for updates from advocacy organizations and government systems to stay informed.

- Respond to requests for public comment. Share your thoughts with decision makers.

- Respond to "requests for proposals" by organizations seeking conference presenters. Present at conferences. Attend conferences and provide feedback about the level of autistic representation.

- Form new groups, events, or organizations.

Academia and Research

This is an area with critical need. Most research about autistic people isn't actually performed by autistic people. Consequently, most research doesn't focus on topics that the autistic community feels are important. If you're in a program of higher learning, reach out to the autistic community to see how you can make a difference.

Boards and Commissions

- *Disability advocacy board of directors.* These roles typically include at least one meeting per month and may be more frequent. In this role, board members are able to influence the direction of advocacy organizations.

- *Government commissions and workgroups* are people who work together to work towards predetermined goals. In this role, you're able to influence government policy.

Education Advocacy

- *Parent-Teacher Associations (PTAs)*: There's more to the PTA than bake sales and parties. Most schools offer behind-the-scenes opportunities that benefit our children: reading to children, having children read to us, helping in the library, sitting with kids in the cafeteria, speaking at career days. The PTA is often involved with school performances and events in which disabled students are less likely to participate. Offer guidance to ensure these programs are accessible for all students.

- *Advisory Committees*: I don't wanna brag but… Okay, yes I do. (*Meghan, here!*) Our school district has a Special Education Advisory Committee and I'm one of their newest members! This type of committee isn't uniform across the nation, but there are plenty of ways to let your voice be heard just by going to public meetings and sitting on various advisory committees in your school district.

- *School Board*: These positions are highly politicized and aren't for everyone. In the past few years, I've seen these members take real abuse. But if you're up for the challenge, we *need* more school board members who are focused on inclusion and trauma-informed practices.

Leadership Education in Neurodevelopmental and Related Disabilities (LEND)

This is a one-year fellowship program in almost every state in which disabled people and parents of disabled children can work alongside upcoming doctors and professionals. Participants of this program receive interdisciplinary training, share their own perspectives, and gain a broader understanding of the issues disabled people and families face. They also learn about policy advocacy.

Parent Mentoring

This type of work can be frustrating. Mentoring parents is not for everyone, and it can be done in different ways. Some people join large groups. Others prefer a more personal approach. Asiatu Lawoyin uses their public platforms to educate and also has a coaching business for one-to-one mentorship. Many other advocates do the same.

Partners in Policymaking (PiP)

This is a year-long state-level program for disabled adults and parents of disabled children. Participants attend advocacy training, build relationships with state leaders, and gain a better understanding of the legislative process.

Peer Mentoring Programs

- Margo Izzo and LeDerick Horne talk about "the path to disability pride" in their book *Empowering Students with Hidden Disabilities* (2016). In isolation, disabled people can experience shame because they often think they're the only ones going through these struggles. Oftentimes they'll reject support, especially as young adults.

  When young people connect with others in the disability community, they're more likely to accept the support they deserve, thus increasing their likelihood of success (in whatever they choose to do). These types of peer mentoring programs are found in colleges and communities across the world. If this interests you, either find one or grab a friend to start one yourself.

- In Australia, the I CAN Network (2022) has been wildly successful as an autistic–autistic mentoring program. Founded in 2013 by an autistic young adult, the I CAN Network is now Australia's largest provider of autistic-led group mentoring programs, training and consultancy, with a team who are all in paid positions.

It's so important for autistic young people to have connections to autistic peers and mentors and know that they are not alone. The not-for-profit I CAN Network provides autistic-led mentoring to thousands of young people ages 8–22 via school-based programs in Australia and online group mentoring (open internationally) each year, including peer-based interest groups and groups for teens who identify as autistic/LGBTIQA+.

Specialty Areas

If big groups are too all-over-the-place for you, there are several specialty areas that could use a person such as yourself. For instance, there aren't enough resources available to help parents navigate the IEP process. There are a few great websites, but parents often need individualized help. Aaron Wright is a parent advocate who uses his platform to empower other parents. Wrightslaw is another organization dedicated to helping in this specific niche. If you're great at deciphering codes, mandates, and laws, this type of work is greatly needed.

Writing

We weren't professional writers until this book was published. We didn't go to school for journalism or take advanced courses in literature. We simply had something to say and started sharing. We started telling our stories and connecting with other people who shared our interest.

Autistic Leadership: Occupy Spaces That Weren't Meant for You

Jules, here. My view of leadership is largely influenced by my ancestors and culture. My great-grandmother Cecilia Robinson was the first woman to serve on the Fond Du Lac Reservation Business Council, which was both an example of traditional matriarchal leadership and ahead of the colonial times. Leadership is a responsibility and an honor.

While our society often advocates for inclusion of disabled people, disabled people are often left out of leadership roles. Rather than presuming competence, we presume that autistic people are unable to successfully lead, when they may in fact need support or accommodations in some areas. In order to achieve our goal of meaningful inclusion, we must include autistic people in leadership positions, ensure these positions are more accessible, and provide appropriate support to those who need it.

I want to close this chapter by sharing that this book title has another meaning to me.

Policy work is often referred to as taking place on "the hill."

Autistic people are dying because of bad decisions being made on the hill.

Autistic people must be heard while legislators make policy decisions that impact our lives. We need autistic people to get involved in creating change in our communities, whether it's writing a letter to a corporation or attending school board meetings or testifying to legislators.

Afterword

— BY JILLIAN NELSON —

// "You are writing the afterword for the book."
       I was thrilled when Jules voluntold me that I would be given the last word in such an important conversation, as this is in fact a hill I have died a thousand deaths on. And let's be honest, I'm spicy autistic and love getting the last word.

As an autistic disability rights lobbyist, I spend a lot of time filling rooms with words, but I don't often get to fill pages of a book. So, I set out to do this the same way I take on political strategizing, with a gigantic idea and a ton of research—I knew the people and the places and the things that needed talking about, so I started simple: by looking up the definition of afterword:

> An afterword is a statement on the entire narrative, and it is frequently told from a different perspective and period of time.
> (MasterClass 2021)

This is fitting—my perspective is quite different as I am not a parent like Jules and Meghan and I joined this community with my diagnosis over 18 years ago, long before autism had lodged itself in either author's vocabulary... As such I feel like I am in a different time period. When I was diagnosed, the rates of autism were six in a thousand kids and not a single book about adults with autism existed. There was no community outside of parents and it was actually seven years before I met another autistic woman and it was Temple Grandin (not exactly new BFF material). As someone with my tenure in diagnosis, I have seen growth beyond my wildest imagination, I have lived through the shift from pathology to culture and community, I have seen research change from causation and cure to access and support, and I have watched a garden of pride and diversity bloom.

This book is the first of its kind (trust me I know, I also curate an autism bookstore), but this conversation has been happening for decades, just not with the insight and understanding this work sheds on the delicate topic of "you're not like my child."

This conversation started in church basement support groups before taking up digital space on AOL message boards, then we moved to Angelfire blogs and chat rooms and yearly conferences about autism...until we came to the current landscape of Facebook groups, meetups, walks, and more conferences than I could imagine attending. Though the spaces and the time changed, each battlefield has one thing in common—parents vs. self-advocates. No matter which venue, it is always flooded with generation after generation of new autistic adults earning battle scars of trauma as we wage war trying to make a difference for future generations.

Some of my earliest memories as a newly diagnosed autistic adult was trying to find a community and being faced with hordes of autism moms telling me that my life experience and my identity and my perspective were wrong, invalid, harmful, and, in a few conversations, retarded. This set the tone for my own reckoning with my new label and trying to understand and accept myself, and set a very solid foundation of posttraumatic stress disorder (PTSD).

I wish I could say that this has changed, but as recently as yesterday these fights are still a regular occurrence, and as we have read in all the pages that came before this, an unnecessary tradition in our community—and one that it is time to end.

In all the fighting we lost sight of the two most important facts: both groups want a better world for autistic kids *and* autistic kids grow up to be autistic adults.

The fights exist between these factions not because of us, or because of them, but because the world we live in is not made for autistic people. Autistically we move through our daily lives facing sensory hurricanes, social booby-traps, and executive dysfunction time bombs...the parents are doing everything they know how to create shelters to protect their children from these hidden attacks...but I think we can agree there are places that we (both autistic children and autistic adults) should be able to feel safe: in our homes, our classrooms, with our community.

Meghan and Jules talked about how they created unity in a space where there was discord. My hope is that as a community we can learn from them and find the power in together. The power of creating a community and forging an autistic culture. The power is in knowledge and education and lived experience. Turns out autistic adults have a lot of knowledge about being autistic kids... and we even know some stuff about sensory challenges and executive function! Even better—we want to share our experiences. And at the same time examine and accept that with great power comes great responsibility (thanks Spider-Man!). The power that the allistic parents of autistic children bring is something very unique but just as valuable—you bring a privilege we don't have. Being able to navigate this world without a disability means that you can choose to be the emcee of the show and call attention to the value autistic adults bring to the table. You have the power to center autistic voices (no matter how we choose to use them, whether verbally or using augmentative and alternative communication, AAC), demand our seats at tables, defend our integrity, and help us get the accommodations we deserve and too often have to fight for.

You have the power to normalize this level of inclusion and respect.

When I see parents and autistics fighting, most of the time I can see the same end goal—the better life for the autism community. Somewhere in all the trauma and all the fear, we forget that.

I often ask parents in that moment if they would want someone to treat their child this way or speak to them disrespectfully or discredit their feelings when they are an adult. The answer has unanimously been, "No, absolutely not." Parents know what they want for their kids' futures—they want them to be respected and valued and loved... We can guarantee that happens by how we treat autistic adults *today*.

As parents, each time you make the choice to support adults openly and visibly, you are telling your child that when they grow up they can do anything they want and it's reasonable to believe there will be people to support them so that they can exist proudly and authentically, autistically as themself. The more you show them this, the more they will know. After all, repetition and consistency are everything in teaching autistic kids!

When I started my career in the nonprofit world, I set my goal as "change the world." I didn't know what that looked like, but I knew that I wanted to make the world better for every autistic person that came after me. I learned quickly that being a radical feminist, queer, polyamorous leftist autistic adult was not going to sit well with the cool kids in the parent and professional autism community. So I learned how to mask, I hid the radical parts of myself, I concealed anything that wouldn't make them wish that their children would grow up to be like me, and I presented myself as the new poster child for "successful adult with autism." What I didn't realize at that time was that I was internalizing ableism and allowing the thinly drawn margins of what was acceptable to dictate who I could be as an autistic leader.

Even though I didn't see it as it was happening, this had giant impacts on my mental health and my self-esteem because I was spending most of my time being something I wasn't, and as such I was also teaching other autistic people that their true self wasn't okay and that success could be theirs if they could learn to play the game right. I hold a lot of guilt for that message, but in the spaces with the people that held all the keys, this is what I had been expected to do if I wanted to be successful, even in spaces that were supposed to be focused on helping people with autism succeed... I didn't know there was another way yet.

Five years ago, I came to work at my current organization. I finally found a freedom to let that mask melt away and a space where being my true authentic autistic self was the best tool I had for building bridges, creating change, and helping others. It was there that I finally figured out that there are a thousand ways to be autistic and that I had the freedom to exist exactly as I am, even if that was constantly changing! Within that freedom I found something I had been chasing my entire adult life—success—and the ability to change the world (well, at least Minnesota legislation and the minds of people I speak to in trainings... but it's a start!).

The unspoken expectation that adult advocates become the "poster child" within the community is a sophisticated form of oppression, because not only does it encourage ableism within ourselves but it pits us against each other—if there is only one right way to be autistic, then all the other ways must be wrong, and if we aren't the one that is right, no one will see us and we will fade away without being seen or heard.

Too often the "poster child" concept in our community erases any lens of intersectionality. We have historically been seen as a community collection of young boys, white, probably wearing a polo shirt and playing with trains. The poster of what autism is expected to be erases the concept of fluid gender and sexuality or a collection of skin colors other than one. It erases economic challenges, it hides support needs, and it most certainly does not reflect the reality of systemic racism and queer erasure that is blatant in the disability community.

The only option for our community to thrive and flourish is to stop dying on hills, battling within our own camp. There are larger enemies if we can find the common ground and embrace the concept of stronger together from a disability justice perspective. The disability justice perspective is the idea that we fight for the most marginalized in our community led by the most marginalized in our community. The concept is not that different from triage in a medical setting—we help the most injured first to avoid the worst possible outcome.

If we embrace this concept that everyone should have access to services and supports, no matter what privilege they bring to the table, we are going to improve services for everyone. If we push for all systems to be accessible for the people with the biggest communication and executive function challenges, everyone will have better access. If we normalize inclusion and appropriate supports then no one will have to fight for the bare minimum. We must erase the concept of privilege and social capital as the gatekeepers for a meaningful life for children and adults with autism.

The enemy is not the blunt adult perseverating on applied behavioral analysis (ABA) research, the enemy is not the parent wearing a puzzle piece t-shirt (but please don't), the enemy is the system that makes it so exhausting for families to get in-home supports, it is the bias that creates inequity in IEPs, it is the administrative burden that makes county services or social security a multi-year battle. If we fight these systems from the perspective of the community as a whole then we can create a better outcome for everyone.

So it's time—I challenge everyone reading this, both parents and advocates, to put down our swords and hold ourselves accountable for what has happened in the past, but also move forward with forgiveness and humbleness. There is no shame in realizing that you were previously speaking from a less informed place, there is no shame in accepting that we have room to learn and grow still.

I am regularly reaching out to Jules for guidance as I do my own work to unpack my white privilege and grow as an ally to BIPOC autistic people. When we commit to changing ourselves to be the best advocates for what our community needs versus being advocates for the best for ourselves, we find ourselves working not as a solo mission but with the strength of an army, with a voice that is not a whisper but with a booming volume that cannot be ignored. If we come together as a united community, what we can accomplish and what we can change is immeasurable.

Finding our community and our unity isn't just something for the battlefields, but also something we can find in friendship. I am the strongest version of myself because of the friendships I surround myself with. While a great number of them are other adults like me, I am also grateful to share loving and caring relationships with many parents of children like me.

When we find that space to value and treasure one another beyond the transactional model of "working" spaces then we find a brilliantly beautiful level of understanding and support. Whether they learn from me as they watch me connect with their children over story time and parallel play, or I am supported by them through a hellscape of paperwork regarding disability benefits, or we just enjoy one another's company over cocktails or food...we become stronger, healthier, wiser, more supported because we are together. Dare I say, we do better...and as a wise senator in Minnesota once said, "We all do better when we all do better" (Paul Wellstone).

References

Ackerman, Mikhaela (May 20, 2018) "Monkey Bars—How Grief Impacted My Autism." Edge of the Playground. Accessed on April 15, 2021 at https://edgeoftheplayground.com/2018/05/20/monkey-bars-how-grief-impacted-my-autism

Ackerman Willis, Mary Lynn and Mikhaela Ackerman (2019) *The Edge of the Playground: Two Stories, One Journey—A Mother and Daughter's Memoir of Autism from Childhood to Adulthood.* Edge of the Playground.

Agony Autie (May 29, 2018) "What Is Autism to You?" Accessed on July 23, 2021 at www.youtube.com/watch?v=H8hHGIJKf3o

Allnutt, Jack and others (July 23, 2019) "Age Appropriate Education." Reach Every Voice. Accessed on August 6, 2021 at www.reacheveryvoice.org/single-post/2019/07/23/age-appropriate-education

American Council on Aging (January 2021) "Medicaid Estate Recovery Programs: When Medicaid Can and Cannot Take One's Home." American Council on Aging. Accessed on November 13, 2021 at www.medicaidplanningassistance.org/can-medicaid-take-my-home

ASAN (Autistic Self Advocacy Network) (2022) "2022 Anti-Filicide Toolkit." Accessed on March 30, 2022 at https://autisticadvocacy.org/projects/community/mourning/anti-filicide

AUSM (Autism Society of Minnesota) (September 28, 2019) *Autism Society of Minnesota Testimony to Deadly Force Encounters Hearing.* Accessed on August 11, 2021 at https://dps.mn.gov/divisions/co/working-group/Documents/Autism%20Society%20of%20MN%20-%20Testimony%20for%20Deadly%20Force%202019.pdf

Autism Speaks (2006) *Autism Every Day.* Documentary.

Autism Speaks (2009) "I Am Autism." Television advertisement.

Autism Speaks (2014) *100 Day Kit for Newly Diagnosed Families of Young Children.* Princeton, NJ: Autism Speaks.

Autism Speaks (2020) *Annual Report April 2019–March 2020.* Accessed on July 5, 2021 at www.autismspeaks.org/sites/default/files/2020_annual_report.pdf

Ballou, Emily Paige (February 6, 2018) "What the Neurodiversity Movement Does—and Doesn't—Offer." Thinking Person's Guide to Autism. Accessed on July 4, 2021 at www.thinkingautismguide.com/2018/02/what-neurodiversity-movement-doesand.html

Bilokonsky, Mykola (2021) "How to Talk about Autism Respectfully: A Field Guide for Journalists, Educators, Doctors, and Anyone Else Who Wants to Know How to Better Communicate About Autism." Public Neurodiversity Support Center. Accessed on December 31, 2021 at https://coda.io/@mykola-bilokonsky/public-neurodiversity-support-center/how-to-talk-about-autism-respectfully-84

Broderick, Alicia A. and Robin Roscigno (2021) "Autism, Inc.: The autism industrial complex." *Journal of Disability Studies in Education*, https://doi.org/10.1163/25888803-bja10008

Brown, Lydia X.Z. (last updated November 16, 2021) "Ableism/Language." Autistic Hoya. Last accessed on March 30, 2021 at www.autistichoya.com/p/ableist-words-and-terms-to-avoid.html

Burgess, Rebecca (March 5, 2019) "Understanding the Spectrum—A Comic Strip Explanation." The Art of Autism. Accessed on May 17, 2021 at https://the-art-of-autism.com/understanding-the-spectrum-a-comic-strip-explanation

CDC (Centers for Disease Control and Prevention) (2019) "Increase in Developmental Disabilities." Centers for Disease Control and Prevention. Accessed on August 4, 2021 at www.cdc.gov/ncbddd/developmentaldisabilities/features/increase-in-developmental-disabilities.html

CDC (Centers for Disease Control and Prevention) (March 27, 2020) "Prevalence of Autism Spectrum Disorder among Children Aged 8 Years—Autism and Developmental Disabilities Monitoring Network, 11 Sites, United States, 2016." Centers for Disease Control and Prevention. Accessed on August 1, 2021 at www.cdc.gov/mmwr/volumes/69/ss/ss6904a1.htm

Cevik, Kerima (August 3, 2019) "On the Dangers of Faux Solutions to Catastrophic Encounters with Law Enforcement." Intersected. Accessed on August 11, 2021 at http://intersecteddisability.blogspot.com/2019/08/on-dangers-of-faux-solutions-to.html

Charlton, James (2000) *Nothing about Us without Us: Disability, Oppression, and Empowerment.* Berkeley, CA: University of California Press.

Craft, Samantha (2020) "Samantha Craft's Autistic Traits Checklist." Spectrum Suite. Accessed on August 9, 2021 at www.myspectrumsuite.com/samantha-crafts-autistic-traits-checklist

Crenshaw, Kimberlé (1989) "Demarginalizing the intersection of race and sex: A Black feminist critique of antidiscrimination doctrine, feminist theory and antiracist politics." *University of Chicago Legal Forum 1989*, 1, Article 8.

Crompton, C.J., M. Sharp, H. Axbey, S. Fletcher-Watson, E.G. Flynn and D. Ropar (2020) "Neurotype-matching, but not being autistic, influences self and observer ratings of interpersonal rapport." *Frontiers in Psychology 11*, 586171, https://doi.org/10.3389/fpsyg.2020.586171

Cross, Terry L. (1997) "Relational Worldview Model." Suicide Prevention Resource Center, National Indian Child Welfare Association. Accessed on August 10, 2021 at www.sprc.org/sites/default/files/resource-program/Relational-Worldview-Model.pdf

Delahooke, Mona (2019) *Beyond Behaviors: Using Brain Science to Understand and Solve Children's Behavioral Challenges*. Eau Claire, WI: PESI Publishing & Media.

DIS (Disability Intersectionality Summit) (2021) "Places to Start." Accessed on August 8, 2021 at www.disabilityintersectionalitysummit.com/places-to-start

Disability Day of Mourning (updated 2021) "Remembering People with Disabilities Murdered by their Families." Accessed on August 15, 2021 at https://disability-memorial.org

Eggerston, Laura (2010) "Lancet retracts 12-year-old article linking autism to MMR vaccines." *CMAJ 182*, 4, 199–200.

Farahar, Chloe and Annette Foster (2021) "#AutisticsInAcademia." In N. Brown (ed.) *Lived Experiences of Ableism in Academia: Strategies for Inclusion in Higher Education*. Bristol: Policy Press.

FCV: Finding Cooper's Voice (November 14, 2017) "The Last Time We Believe This Is Going to Be Okay." YouTube: Finding Cooper's Voice. Accessed on June 20, 2021 at https://youtu.be/uCZmSEOynVo

FDA (U.S. Food and Drug Administration) (April 17, 2019) "Be Aware of Potentially Dangerous Products and Therapies that Claim to Treat Autism." Accessed on July 1, 2021 at www.fda.gov/consumers/consumer-updates/be-aware-potentially-dangerous-products-and-therapies-claim-treat-autism

FNEHIN (First Nations Environmental Health Innovation Network) (July 2014) "Cyclical Worldview: Understanding Environmental Health from a First Nations Perspective." Accessed on August 10, 2021 at http://lfs-indigenous.sites.olt.ubc.ca/files/2014/07/CyclicalWorldviewEngFinal.pdf

Foundations for Divergent Minds (n.d.) "What is Neurodiversity?" Divergent Minds. Accessed on August 3, 2021 at www.divergentminds.org/understanding-neurodiversity

Gernsbacher, Morton Ann and Melanie Yergeau (2019) "Empirical failures of the claim that autistic people lack a theory of mind." *Archives of Scientific Psychology* 7, 1, 102–118.

Gray, Alison J. (2011) "Worldviews." *International Psychiatry 8*, 3, 58–60.

Higashida, Naoki, David Mitchell, and Keiko Yoshida (2013) *The Reason I Jump: One Boy's Voice from the Silence of Autism*. New York: Random House.

Hunja, Ellie (June 12, 2021) "Non-Autistic Parents: Why We Should Get Comfortable with Being Uncomfortable." Not an Autism Mom. Accessed on July 20, 2021 at https://notanautismmom.com/2021/06/12/non-autistic-parents-why-we-should-get-comfortable-with-being-uncomfortable

I CAN Network (2022) "Autistic-Led Services for Young People and Organizations." Last accessed on March 30, 2022 at https://icannetwork.online

Izzo, Margo Vreeburg and LeDerick Horne (2016) *Empowering Students with Hidden Disabilities: A Path to Pride and Success*. Baltimore, MD: Paul H. Brookes Publishing.

Jallow, Lovette (November 28, 2020) "Being a Black Woman in Sweden—Author-Talk with Lovette Jallow 'Stranger in White Spaces.'" Accessed on July 5, 2021 at https://youtu.be/xScapi8xcNU

Kedar, Ido (2012) *Ido in Autismland: Climbing Out of Autism's Silent Prison.* [Self-published.]

Kingsley, Emily Perl (1987) "Welcome to Holland." Accessed on May 2, 2022 at www.dsasc.ca/uploads/8/5/3/9/8539131/welcome_to_holland.pdf

Litton Tidd, Jennifer (May 18, 2021) "What is the Difference between the Medical and Social Models of Disability and Why Does It Matter?" Alliance Against Seclusion and Restraint. Accessed on August 7, 2021 at https://endseclusion.org/2021/05/18/what-is-the-difference-between-the-medical-and-social-models-of-disability-and-why-does-it-matter

Lives in the Balance (2021) "Resources for Advocators." Lives in the Balance. Accessed on September 1, 2021 at https://livesinthebalance.org/advocacy/resources-for-advocators

Lynch, C.L. (2019) "Person-First Language: What Is It and When Not to Use It." NeuroClastic. Accessed on June 4, 2021 at https://neuroclastic.com/2019/04/19/person-first

MasterClass (2021) "Learn About Epilogue in Writing: Definition, Examples, and How to Write an Epilogue in 4 Steps." MasterClass. Accessed on May 2, 2022 at www.masterclass.com/articles/writing-101-what-is-an-epilogue#what-is-the-definition-of-epilogue

Milton, Damian (2012) "On the ontological status of autism: The 'double empathy problem.'" *Disability & Society* 27, 6, 883–887.

NAEYC (National Association for the Education of Young Children) (2020a) "DAP: Creating a Caring, Equitable Community of Learners." Accessed on May 3, 2021 at www.naeyc.org/resources/position-statements/dap/creating-community

NAEYC (National Association for the Education of Young Children) (2020b) "DAP: Defining Developmentally Appropriate Practice." Accessed on July 25, 2021 at www.naeyc.org/resources/position-statements/dap/definition

NCAI (National Congress of American Indians) (February 2018) "Violence against American Indian and Alaska Native Women." Accessed on August 12, 2021 at www.ncai.org/policy-research-center/research-data/prc-publications/VAWA_Data_Brief__FINAL_2_1_2018.pdf

Norris, Heather (2014) "Colonialism and the rupturing of Indigenous worldviews of impairment and relational interdependence: A beginning dialogue towards reclamation and social transformation." *Critical Disability Discourse/Discours Critiques dans le Champ du Handicap* 6, 53–79.

Not an Autism Mom (July 20, 2020) "100-ish Books on Autism and Neurodiversity." Accessed on June 3, 2021 at https://notanautismmom.com/2020/07/20/autism-books

Not an Autism Mom (May 1, 2021) "Free Printable List of Autism-Positive Books for New Parents." Accessed on July 15, 2021 at https://notanautismmom.com/2021/05/01/free-printable-list-of-autism-positive-books-for-new-parents

OJP (Office of Justice Programs) (1995) "Sexual Abuse Interview for Those with Developmental Disabilities." Accessed on September 12, 2021 at www.ojp.gov/ncjrs/virtual-library/abstracts/sexual-abuse-interview-those-developmental-disabilities

OJP–OVC (Office of Justice Programs–Office for Victims of Crime) (June 2014) "Responding to Transgender Victims of Sexual Assault." Accessed on August 12, 2021 at https://ovc.ojp.gov/sites/g/files/xyckuh226/files/pubs/forge/sexual_numbers.html

Perry, David (2017) *The Ruderman White Paper: On Media Coverage of the Murder of People with Disabilities by Their Caregivers.* Ruderman Family Foundation. Accessed on April 24, 2022 at https://rudermanfoundation.org/wp-content/uploads/2017/08/Murders-by-Caregivers-WP_final_final.pdf

Piper, Reese (November 30, 2017) "'I Thought I Was Lazy': The Invisible Day-to-Day Struggle for Autistic Women." Medium. Accessed on August 8, 2021 at https://medium.com/the-establishment/i-thought-i-was-lazy-the-invisible-day-to-day-struggle-for-autistic-women-6268515175f3

Prizant, Barry (2015) *Uniquely Human: A Different Way of Seeing Autism.* New York: Simon & Schuster Paperbacks.

Reiland, Eve (2021) "The Influence Network of Autism Speaks That Silenced Autistic People." International Badass Activists. Accessed on August 1, 2021 at https://americanbadassactivists.wordpress.com/2021/03/18/the-influence-network-of-autism-speaks

REV (Reach Every Voice) (2021) Accessible Academics: Strategies for Adapting Age-Appropriate Academics for Non-Speaking Students.

Reyes, Philip (February 11, 2021) "Top 10 Things You Should Know about Apraxia According to a Nonspeaker." NeuroClastic. Accessed on August 8, 2021 at https://neuroclastic.com/2021/02/11/top-10-things-you-should-know-about-apraxia-according-to-an-apraxic

Rose, Kieran (May 21, 2018) "An Autistic Burnout." The Autistic Advocate. Accessed on April 17, 2021 at https://theautisticadvocate.com/2018/05/an-autistic-burnout

Sankar, Tejas Rao and others (February 11, 2021) "Nonspeaker Perspectives on Representation." NeuroClastic. Accessed on August 7, 2021 at https://neuroclastic.com/2021/02/11/nonspeaker-perspectives-on-representation

Sequenzia, Amy (November 20, 2017) "Parenting and Advocating with Autistic Children." AWN: Autistic Women & Nonbinary Network. Accessed on August 4, 2021 at https://awnnetwork.org/parenting-advocating-autistic-children

Silberman, Steve (2015) *NeuroTribes: The Legacy of Autism and the Future of Neurodiversity.* New York: Avery.

Simon, Stephanie (February 10, 2015) "No Profit Left Behind." Politico. Accessed on August 1, 2021 at www.politico.com/story/2015/02/pearson-education-115026

Sinclair, Jim (1993) "Don't Mourn for Us." *Our Voice 1*, 3. Accessed on August 5, 2021 at https://philosophy.ucsc.edu/SinclairDontMournForUs.pdf

Sins Invalid (September 17, 2015) "10 Principles of Disability Justice." Last accessed on March 31, 2022 at www.sinsinvalid.org/blog/10-principles-of-disability-justice

Stroud, Barbara (July 19, 2021) "Dr. Barbara Stroud Full Interview." YouTube Channel Not an Autism Mom. Accessed on July 23, 2021 at https://youtu.be/rxV2iS8m3k0

Thornton, Cheyenne (April 18, 2021) "ABA for Creating Masking Black Autistics." NeuroClastic. Accessed on August 5, 2021 at https://neuroclastic.com/aba-for-creating-masking-black-autistics

Tucker, Ethan (June 26, 2017) "Hear My Voice, Too." Reach Every Voice. Accessed on August 6, 2021 at www.reacheveryvoice.org/single-post/2017/06/23/untitled

Tziavaras, William (June 23, 2021) "Fleeing the World of Silence." International Association for Spelling as Communication (I-ASC). Accessed on August 7, 2021 at https://i-asc.org/fleeing-the-world-of-silence

Tziavaras, William and Giorgena Sarantopoulos (May 27, 2020) "Six Things You Should Know about Apraxia: What It's Like & What We *Think* We Know." International Association for Spelling as Communication (I-ASC). Accessed on August 5, 2021 at https://i-asc.org/six-things-you-should-know-about-apraxia

Ujima (The National Center on Violence Against Women in the Black Community) (December 2018) "Black Women and Sexual Assault." Accessed on August 12, 2021 at https://ujimacommunity.org/wp-content/uploads/2018/12/Ujima-Womens-Violence-Stats-v7.4-1.pdf

Verified Market Research (VMR) (September 2020) "Autism Spectrum Disorders Market Size and Forecast." Accessed on August 13, 2021 at www.verifiedmarketresearch.com/product/autism-spectrum-disorders-market

Walker, Nick (2021) *Neuroqueer Heresies: Notes on the Neurodiversity Paradigm, Autistic Empowerment, and Postnormal Possibilities*. Fort Worth, TX: Autonomous Press.

Williams, Kat (April 4, 2019) "The Fallacy of Functioning Labels." National Centre for Mental Health (NCMH). Accessed on July 1, 2021 at www.ncmh.info/2019/04/04/fallacy-functioning-labels

xMinds (2020) "Nonspeaking Autistic Students Resources." Accessed on August 4, 2021 at https://xminds.org/Nonspeaking-Autistics